MW01502976

Secrets To Growing Your Veterinary Practice In The New Economy

By Steve Maughan & Dean Biggs

ISBN: 1456366912
ISBN-13: 978-1456366919

DEDICATION

For the women who make what we do possible—our wives, Stephanie and Emma—and the girls who inspire us—our beautiful daughters, Evangeline, Pippa, and Charlotte.

CONTENTS

Section 3: Client Retention
(Putting a Fence around Your Clients: How to keep your clients happy, engaged, and resistant to approaches from other practices!)

Section 4: Client Revenue
(Increasing the Value of Each Client: How to increase your profits without increasing the number of clients you serve!)

Section 5: Laying the Foundations for Success
(Developing the Culture: Creating an environment for everyday success in your veterinary practice!)

Section 6: Resources

ACKNOWLEDGMENTS

Our grateful thanks go first to our Lord and Savior, Jesus Christ, through whom all things are possible and without whom we would never have met and never written this book. In an uncertain World, You are the only real certainty.

To Nick Nanton, Chris Hurn, Travis Miller, Jimmy Vee, Nigel Worral and all the other Orlando-based entrepreneurs who have inspired us to bring a whole new world to veterinary practice owners.

To our inspirational mentors, "Millionaire Maker" Dan Kennedy, Bill Glazer, Michael Gerber, the late Gary Halbert, John Carlton, Gary Bencivenga, Rich Scheffren, Bob Bly, Clayton Makepeace, Michael Fortin, Frank Kern, Ryan Deiss, and all the other gurus whose teachings have inspired our programs.

To George Gunn and Bob Jones for their continuous support and encouragement over many years.

To Dr. Rick Marrinson and his team at Longwood Veterinary Clinic for all your help and support and for making what we do worthwhile.

To all our veterinary practice clients for your continued support and for daring to be different.

And finally, to all the Veterinary Practice Owners out there who ensure that our pets are looked after—for the long hours you work and your dedication to veterinary medicine, for keeping going when times are tough and the rewards of your work are not always matched financially—this book is for you.

FOREWORD

BY ROBERT W. JONES
HEAD, INTERNATIONAL, NOVARTIS ANIMAL HEALTH

I never really wanted to be a veterinarian. I am still not a veterinarian but by choice I have been around animals, large and small, and in the animal health business my whole life. Looking back, when choosing an educational path in the 70s, I chose animal nutrition because the veterinarians that came to our ranch or that we took the dogs to never seemed to prosper. Now I know why.

A few pages from now, you'll read how one of the authors, Steve Maughan, has worked with animal health companies in assessing their businesses around the world. I was one of the guys that benefitted from Steve's intellect and have lost count of how many evaluations we have done together. I count myself lucky to have worked with Steve and thoroughly enjoyed the challenge of trying to figure out why things work the way they do in the animal health and the veterinary industries.

One visit I made to a veterinary clinic in the US several years ago drove home the notion that the New Economy presents a clear and present danger to the clinic-owning veterinarian. With the sales representative sitting next to me in the veterinarian's cluttered office, he showed us a pile of faxes from an Internet pharmacy requesting his signature so they could process orders for his customers. When asked what he was doing about these "customers," the answer was that he would not fight "it" anymore and would just sign them.

"It" meant competition, the Internet, the New Economy. He just gave up. More likely, he just didn't know what to do about it.

Around the world, I am often amazed how many veterinarians feel in their bones that helping animals and making money at it are mutually exclusive goals: you can't (or shouldn't) do both. Just cover your costs, treat the animals, save the pet owner money.

The fact that you are reading this book means that you are likely not in this group. You understand that the purpose of a business is to make money now and into the future and that by doing so, you will be able to provide your pet-owning customers with the best possible experience—better than the competitors down the road, in the next town, or on the Internet.

This book by Steve and Dean will help you do this, showing you how to reach your goals and grow your practice in the New Economy. In this easy to read book, you'll find secrets that most veterinarians, probably most small business owners, don't know. You'll learn how to attract new clients, how to segment them, and how to use the Internet and tools like Google® to help your practice grow and prosper.

The tips and suggestions on retaining the clients you already have are practical and are based on communication. Finally, their guidance on increasing the value of each client is unambiguous and implementable.

So if you want to prosper, if you want to be different from those veterinarians in the 70's, if you want to grow your practice in the most challenging and disruptive economic times many of us have known, follow Steve and Dean's advice.

Robert W. Jones
Head, International
Novartis Animal Health

P.S. If you think you can't do the things Steve and Dean recommend—"too much marketing, I'm a vet, after all"—find that unique person in your practice and let them be the catalyst for your growth.

CHAPTER 1
INTRODUCTION

So often times it happens that we live our lives in chains
And we never even know we have the key.

–Lyrics from Already Gone, performed by the Eagles on their 1974 Album *On the Border*

Let us tell you a story. For the past fifteen years, Steve Maughan has helped multinational animal health companies plan their sales and marketing strategies. This has taken him to over thirty-five countries, where he has studied animal health industries so that he can develop better sales and marketing plans for his clients.

As part of this work, Steve has analyzed thousands of veterinary practices so as to identify their sales potential. He has constantly been amazed at the variation in sales from one practice to another. Why was one practice struggling to stay in business when a similar practice nearby was booming? What was the "secret sauce" that a few practices had discovered that was allowing them to grow relentlessly no matter what was happening to the economy?

These questions seemed important to Steve, and he set out to discover the common success factors and distill them into core principles that could be applied to any veterinary practice.

During his search, he encountered Dean Biggs, an expert in small business marketing. Steve was amazed at the results Dean had achieved with his online and offline marketing. In one direct mail campaign, for example, Dean had managed to get a 16.7% response rate—about ten times what Steve would have expected.

Dean was also a dog lover, so it wasn't too difficult for Steve to persuade him that they should work together to create products and services that could accelerate the growth of veterinary practices. And so Veterinary Practice Profits was born.

Neither of us is a veterinarian, but that's OK, because we're not going to teach you veterinary medicine. In fact, it's more than OK. Since we are not veterinarians, we do not have a lot of the social and institutional conditioning and thought processes that limit some veterinary consultants and management trainers.

What we offer are strategies new to most veterinarians that will build your practice in what many experts are now calling a New Economy. We'll discuss what the New Economy is and what it means to you as a veterinarian in the next chapter. First, though, think back, and answer this question:

Why Did You Become a Veterinarian?

Most of you will say that you were attracted to the profession because you love animals. No doubt the training you received at veterinary school gave you the skills you needed to land your first job and start working as a veterinarian. At first you were happy just to be working in animal health but inevitably, professional maturity brought changes in your goals. After a couple of years working, you may well have started to dream of owning your own practice.

After all, you're a great veterinarian, so why shouldn't you work for yourself and cut out the middle man (i.e. the practice owner)? As a veterinarian, owning your own practice certainly seems the most logical path to financial freedom.

Let's suppose you have achieved your dream of owning your very own veterinary practice, and you want it to be successful. Now what? Now it needs to grow, because if it's not growing, it's dying. So how do you grow your practice?

In order for a practice to be successful, the owner's perspective needs to change from that of "doer" to that of "owner." Without the right coaching, this can be tough, because veterinary schools do not put any emphasis on teaching entrepreneurial skills.

A new practice owner therefore simply hopes that the practice will grow—that passing traffic will see the new office and drop by; that the local community will want and welcome a new vet; that friends and family will spread the word about the talented, dedicated, service-oriented new veterinarian.

More often than not, it turns out that having an office presence will bring in some clients, and with luck, those few clients will be enough to pay the bills. But the cold, hard truth is this: in the New Economy, a strategy of hope will never deliver the financial freedom that you desire.

If you would rather not rely on hope to grow your practice, then this book is for you.

If you are looking for some inspiration as you begin your journey in veterinary practice ownership, then this book is for you.

If you have been running a practice for years, but every year feels the same, and your practice drifts along in neutral financially, then this book is for you.

If you have grown your practice to a plateau where it now seems stuck, and you want to find ways to get the edge you need to reignite its growth, then this book is for you.

We suggest you grab a highlighter pen, find a quiet place to read and switch your cell phone off because whatever your story, whatever your reasons for reading this book, you are about to receive the keys to unlocking the chains that have been holding your practice back from whatever you would like it to become. You just have to use them!

SECTION 1

SIGNPOST TO SUCCESS

Introducing the New Economy
and the skills you will need to
survive and thrive in it!

CHAPTER 2
THE NEW ECONOMY

Business Success in The New Economy will be earned, not given.

–Dan Kennedy (from his book *No B.S. Business Success in The New Economy*)

At the end of 2010, reports on the veterinary industry showed that visits to veterinary practices were down at least 6%, on average, over the previous twelve months. Some veterinary practices may be bucking this trend, but for many others the statistics are even worse and verging on desperate.

Some business experts believe that although we are slowly moving out of the recession, the good old days are gone forever and will be replaced by an emerging New Economy.

So what is the New Economy and how does it affect veterinary practices?

Well, it's pretty clear that we're not going back to the credit card fuelled free-spending economy that contributed to the recession in the first place! Instead, the old housing-boom economy is being replaced with an economy that is much more demanding and much less forgiving.

In the New Economy, every business, including veterinary practices, must a have profound reason for being. You might have dreamed of opening a practice in your favorite part of your country, state, county, or town, but the market cares little for your dreams and ambitions; it is only interested in what it needs and wants.

One reason businesses have struggled in the economic downturn is because too many businesses of the same type are offering the same products and services. The same stores appear every few miles; chain restaurants everywhere serve exactly the same foods.

For example, a survey asked customers coming out of three major office supply chains to turn their backs on the storefront and cover the bags they were carrying. Then they were asked which of the three chains' stores they had just left. Most of them didn't know, because all those stores are the same!

One of our mentors, Dan Kennedy, jokes that they've now run out of new places for Starbucks, so now they're building Starbucks in the Men's Rooms of existing Starbucks! Although Starbucks gets most parts of the business right, even they have been affected by this economy.

Just as many financial experts believe that the stock market and real estate market losses were a natural regression to what they were really worth, the New Economy is redressing the balance of business supply too. There's over-supply of most businesses, and consumers are voting with their feet to choose which ones will survive. In fact, consumers have more power now than ever before, and they're not afraid to use it!

The signs are that consumers are much more value

conscious in this economy than ever before, and they now have zero tolerance for the ordinary and the incompetent! Notice our use of the word *value* and not *price.* Consumers are still willing to pay for value, as we shall see later.

In the New Economy, however, money is being spent much more judiciously, as you no doubt have noticed. Your practice is under more scrutiny than ever before, with clients trying to weigh whether you are worthy to treat their pet and receive their hard-earned dollars!

The truth is this:

There's Never been a more Critical Time for Veterinary Practice Owners!

In the past year or so, we've seen a number of successful, experienced veterinarians, accustomed to rivers of money flowing to them, suddenly finding themselves staring at dry creek beds. In fact, one veterinary practice owner put it this way:

Before the recession, it was impossible to fail; all you had to do was find a halfway decent location, open up, and clients would flood in. Now we've got to work for it!

As you will discover in this book, the single most effective thing you can do to survive and thrive in the New Economy is to be different. After all, if you do the same as every other veterinary practice, then you'll get the same results. Remember, average equates to ordinary; you want to be extraordinary.

The reason many veterinary practices get "price shopped" is because they are offering exactly what a pet owner can find at every other veterinary practice out there. Now, you might argue that vaccinations are pretty much a commodity, and you would be right. But what's more of a commodity than coffee? Yet

Starbucks sells it more expensively and with more customer loyalty than any other coffee shop. Why? They deliver a uniquely desirable experience.

Remember, when what you deliver is perceived as a commodity, even the affluent will shop for the cheapest price. But when you deliver a memorable experience that creates an emotional connection, price is not an issue. Even something as simple as a vaccination can be wrapped in an experience that is worth the extra cost.

Creating a world-class client experience is important because it will set you apart. This is not what most of your competitors will be delivering!

Before we give away the secrets to not only surviving but actually thriving in the New Economy, let's make sure you've got your mind in the right place to succeed.

CHAPTER 3
THE MINDSET TO SUCCEED

Whatever the mind can conceive and believe, the mind can achieve.

–Napoleon Hill

The most successful veterinary practice owners in the United States today did not become successful by chance. They started with a set of beliefs about how to achieve success, and they took action based on those beliefs.

Success has a different meaning to every individual, so before you can begin your journey to a successful practice, or measure how far along the road you are towards having one, you need define what success means to you.

What Does Success Look Like?

Ask yourself this question:

If you work hard building up your veterinary practice, can it be the most successful practice in:

- A one-mile radius of your practice?

- Your Town?
- Your County?
- Your State?
- The USA?
- The World?

The answer you give reveals your mindset.

> ***If you think you can, or you think you can't, you are probably right.***
>
> –Henry Ford

If you truly believe you can have the world's most successful veterinary practice, you most certainly have a success-oriented mindset and are most likely going to be a very successful and wealthy person. On the other hand, if you selected one of the other answers, then you need to answer the follow-up question, which is this:

What Is Stopping You?

Here is a selection of the reasons that people give:

- I don't have the time.
- I don't have the money.
- I don't have the talent.
- I don't have the right staff.

- I don't have the right clients.
- My practice is in the wrong town or the wrong part of town.

In order to make the shift from highly skilled veterinarian to highly successful practice owner, you need to believe that your practice can be as big and successful as you want it to be.

Once you have decided what success means for you, then you need to learn the skills to get you there. In our experience, it isn't lack of clinical expertise that keeps so many veterinary practices from achieving their full potential. It's more often the result of a lack of clear vision or lack of sales, marketing, and business skills to realize the vision.

Goal Setting Is the Master Skill for Life-long Success.

Read any self-help book or any book by a business guru, and undoubtedly you will find at least a mention of and perhaps an entire section devoted to goal setting. Books are written on the subject, and most successful people will freely acknowledge that their success was once a goal scribbled on a piece of paper.

You may have heard of the 1979 Yale goal study or the 1953 Harvard goal study that found only 3% of graduates had written goals. When interviewed several years later, the 3% were found to be earning more than the other 97% combined!

These are great stories that have been used by some legendary self-improvement gurus to demonstrate the power of goal setting. Unfortunately, they are no more than urban myths; those studies never actually took place!

Dominican University in California did do a study, however, in which 149 participants were divided randomly into five groups. Members of four of the groups were asked to write goals, while members of the other group were asked just to think about their goals. The participants were between 23 and 72 years of age and came from a variety of countries including the United States, Belgium, England, India, Australia, and Japan. They included entrepreneurs, educators, healthcare professionals, artists, attorneys, bankers, marketers, human services providers, managers, vice presidents, directors of non-profits, and others.

Participants were asked to pursue a variety of goals over a four-week period: increasing income, increasing productivity, getting organized, enhancing life balance, enhancing performance/achievement, reducing work anxiety, learning a new skill, and completing projects. At the end of the four weeks, participants were asked to rate their progress and the degree to which they had accomplished their goals.

After the results were compiled, one of the main conclusions was that those who wrote their goals accomplished significantly more than those who did not write their goals. While these results are not as powerful as the legendary Harvard/Yale effects, they do give scientific evidence that having written goals will give you an advantage.

Think of the following analogy: when a cargo ship leaves port it has to have a predefined destination, a goal of where it is going, because if it didn't it would just drift along until it reached some random destination or hit something and sank.

Do you want your practice to drift along towards some random place, or sink? Or would you rather have a clear destination in mind and a plan that will get you there?

You Need Goals

Do you have clearly defined written goals for yourself and your practice that you hold yourself accountable to every day?

If not, then you need to set some. If you do have clearly defined written goals but don't feel that you are getting closer to them, make sure they are MUST HAVE goals and not just NICE TO HAVE goals. Taking action is the key to making your goals a reality, and you will only **take action** on your goals when you make them a must in your mind.

There are some fantastic books on goal setting—anything by Brian Tracy is worth reading—but here are our top four tips for setting and achieving your goals specifically in relation to your veterinary practice.

1. **Make a Wish List**

   Make a list of everything you want or dream about having in life. List everything, including material possessions, financial health, physical health, quality of relationships with family and friends, where you want to be spiritually, places you want to visit, skills you would like to learn—everything you want from life in every area of your life.

   Don't hold back here. Think of your dreams as goals without a deadlines. You should be able to come up with dozens of things you want in your life.

2. **Set The Ultimate Goal for Your Practice**

   Now that you know what you want out of life, you need to decide where your practice has to be for you to achieve your goals. To do that, look at the top ten items on your list. If any of them has monetary value (e.g., homes, cars, boats, etc.), write its value next to that item. If there are things that require time (e.g., vacations, learning to play an instrument) write the time value for each of those.

How much profit will it take each year to pay for those things you just valued? Do you need to expand your practice with an extension to your current premises or even a another facility in another part of town? What does the composition of your team need to look like for you to have the time to visit the places you've always dreamed of?

3. **Set the Deadline for Success**

Next, you need to set a deadline for when you are going to have achieved your ultimate goal. We suggest setting smaller goals with intermediate and short-term deadlines to serve as milestones on your route to achieving your ultimate goal. For example, if your deadline for success is three years from now, then you can set milestone goals for two years, twelve months, six months, three months, thirty days, and this week.

4. **Take Action Today**

Decide what steps you can take today to start along the path to achieving your first milestone, and then begin to take those steps!

Just doing this will give you a clearer vision of the direction your practice needs to go. It will also put you ahead of the veterinary practices that would like to be doing better but have no vision of where they need to be.

Of course, while having clearly defined goals for your life and your practice is essential for making your practice a success, there are things you can do to reach your goals more quickly.

Taking the Shortcut to Success

> ***The great majority of people do not achieve unusual success; why would we expect that getting in the same line as them in any endeavor would result in any sort of remarkable success?***
>
> –Earl Nightingale

Most veterinary practices base their marketing and practice-growing strategies on the same models used by 95% of other veterinary practices. When you're starting your own practice, it's very easy to follow what the other practices in your area are doing or to copy the marketing activities of the practice you just left.

The problem in doing this is that most other practices are not doing a great job of marketing or growing. In fact, only the top 5% are really nailing it and consistently growing. We're going to show you how your practice could be in that top 5%.

Didn't you decide to set up your own practice partly because you thought you could do things better than the practice where you had been employed? So doesn't it make sense that the last thing you should be doing is copying what they did?

Earl Nightingale, one of the greatest motivational speakers and educators of our time, said that to be successful in any industry or profession, you should find out what the successful ones were doing and copy that. Or you could look at what the other 95% was doing, and do the exact opposite.

Your takeaway here is that if you want to have an extraordinarily successful practice then you need to be different from the 95% of practices that are ordinary.

> ***If you want to be successful in life, simply watch what most people would do in a given situation, and then do the total opposite—nine times out of ten, you'll receive greater rewards.***
>
> –Earl Nightingale

Our aim is to give you the shortcuts to success, the proven strategies that can make an immediate impact in your practice and catapult your profits and growth way beyond anything you have experienced.

This book will teach you those strategies. The good news for you is that the most veterinary practices either underutilize them or ignore them completely. In fact, even the most successful practices in the United States, while using many of them, will not be using all of them.

This means that if you dare and are prepared to be different from your competition, and if you take these strategies aboard whole-heartedly, you have a real opportunity to make yours the most successful veterinary practice in your area and beyond. We say "and beyond" because once you have implemented some of these strategies in your veterinary business and started to see the results they achieve, you will become excited at the possibilities and want to implement more of them.

Once the success snowball starts to roll, it can take you wherever you want to go, whether that means just one hugely successful practice or an entire chain of them; that's up to you.

The first step, however, is to understand that growing a successful veterinary practice requires a completely different skill set from practicing veterinary medicine. Fortunately, the skills you need can be acquired in a lot less time than you spent becoming a vet. You simply replicate what has been shown to work for very successful veterinary practices (the minority) and adapt some successful marketing strategies from other industries.

In order to develop a successful practice you must come to the realization that you need more than your veterinary medicine skills alone. You must develop yourself into an **Entrepreneurial Veterinarian.**

CHAPTER 4
THE ENTREPRENEURIAL VETERINARIAN

Most entrepreneurs are merely technicians with an entrepreneurial seizure. Most entrepreneurs fail because you are working IN your business rather than ON your business.

–Michael Gerber

In 1985, Michael Gerber wrote a classic book called The E-Myth, which he defined as follows:

> **E-Myth** 'e-, 'mith *n* **1:** the entrepreneurial myth: the myth that most people who start small businesses are entrepreneurs; **2:** the fatal assumption that an individual who understands the technical work of a business can successfully run a business that does that technical work.

The book has two main hypotheses:

1. Technically oriented people starting their own businesses often forget that just as they once had to learn and use their technical expertise, they must also learn to manage the operations of a company.

So just because the fact that you spent years learning to become a veterinarian and then years practicing veterinary medicine doesn't mean that you should expect to have all of the knowledge required to manage a successful veterinary practice.

2. In order to create a business that can be grown, duplicated and thrive even when you're not there, you must create a systems-based business model that produces consistent, predictable results.

In short, being a great veterinarian does not automatically mean that you will have a successful veterinary practice.

The cold hard fact is this:

Veterinarians who are better at marketing—and who create better systems—will have more success than veterinarians who are more clinically skilled!

They will do better because they know how to market themselves, and marketing is an essential skill for growing your practice.

For many veterinarians that's hard to take, but it's true. But as the late Bobby Kennedy once said, "Don't get mad, get even." In other words, you don't have to like the fact that marketing can be more important than skill. You just become a better marketer, because the veterinarian who can deliver the best service and has the best marketing will take the market, period!

Now just in case the word 'marketing' send shivers down your spine, let's just clear something up right now. We know that some veterinarians have been conditioned to believe that marketing and advertising are somehow immoral, unprofessional or even unethical but our view is this:

If you believe that your veterinary practice delivers first class patient care then it's your duty to the pets in your area to let their owners know about it! Not doing so leaves them at the mercy of those that do not adhere to your standards!

Marketing is an entrepreneurial activity and the key to success is to move from being a practicing veterinarian to being an entrepreneurial veterinarian.

Now, if the word *entrepreneur* conjures up an image of making money at the expense of client service and patient care, you can relax. This could not be further from the truth.

Here's our portrait of the *Entrepreneurial Veterinarian*:

- *The veterinarian whose practice delivers a world-class experience for its clients and their pets and a life-sustaining practice for the employees who work there;*
- *The veterinarian who has put systems in place so that the practice runs like clockwork, even when she is not there;*
- *The veterinarian who understands that marketing doesn't depend upon advertising and promotion alone but also requires developing a culture of client attraction and satisfaction;*
- *The veterinarian who is constantly looking for ways to give his practice an edge over the competition;*
- *The veterinarian whose clients eagerly refer their friends and family, because the care their pets receive and the experience they get make it worth every penny it costs;*
- *The veterinarian who is always looking for new ways to grow his practice;*

- *The veterinarian who has control of his practice and knows his numbers;*
- *The veterinarian who knows what he wants and is willing to learn from others to get it;*
- *The veterinarian whose practice is successful apart from her, not because of her.*

The clients of the veterinarian entrepreneur are raving fans who will drive miles past other veterinary practices to get the care they and their pets deserve. The veterinarian entrepreneur is in total control of his destiny, works balanced hours, has little stress, is financially fulfilled, and has a business that will support him in the future.

Although this may sound like a pipe dream, for the most successful practices, this is an everyday reality. The sooner you start to think of yourself as a veterinary **business** owner rather than a veterinary **practice** owner, the sooner you will be making this a reality in your life too.

Becoming an Entrepreneurial Veterinarian is more than just working on your veterinary business as opposed to working in it. It's a mindset.

Veterinary Entrepreneurs Think Differently

As you make the transition from Veterinary Practice Owner to Veterinary Entrepreneur, you will begin to think much differently about your business and very differently from the majority of your peers and competitors.

You see, for the typical veterinary practice owner, the business looks identical now to the way it looked when it opened. Perhaps you have more clients by now, you may have more veterinarians and other team members, and you may even have better equipment so you can offer more modern procedures than when you began. You may have expanded, relocated to new premises, or even opened a second clinic. Fundamentally, however, you are probably still operating the same business and offering the same services to the same sort of clients.

An entrepreneurial veterinarian's business, on the other hand, will look very different from the way it looked when it began. For instance, she isn't relying on just one business activity; she has several other pet-related satellite businesses that orbit around her core veterinary business. She may be offering pet training classes, pet nutrition classes, concierge services, and a pet grooming service. She has several Websites promoting products or services related to veterinary medicine, such as dentistry, or related to pet care, such as dog beds and bowls or grooming and boarding. She might also have pet-related membership clubs and any of several other pet-related ventures.

This does not mean that the entrepreneurial veterinarian has stopped caring about animal health or even stopped practicing veterinary medicine. What it does mean is that he is making the most of his clientele and doing the most for his clients by offering pet-related products and services that they would otherwise have to buy elsewhere, and he is bringing more new clients to his veterinary business by attracting them with non-veterinary goods and services.

The entrepreneurial veterinarian is constantly looking for additional ways to serve pet owners. He knows that the more pet owners he can serve outside his core veterinary business, the more pet owners he will get to serve inside his veterinary business.

In many cases, though, the satellite businesses grow larger than the core business, a sign of huge profit potential in a short time.

The entrepreneurial veterinarian also has strategic alliances with other businesses that share the same customer demographic. These allies could be pet-related, including rescue shelters and pet boutiques, and or not pet-related. For example, a practice with a current (or desired) client base of women 35-55 might partner with a local beauty spa to offer its clients dog-sitting that includes a similar spa experience with the vet's groomer. If the client will bring her dog to you for grooming, there's a very good chance she will let you provide veterinary care too! Joint ventures with appropriate business can be worth their weight in gold so be sure to nurture the ones you make.

It is this sort of entrepreneurial thinking that can give you a distinct advantage over your competitors by allowing you to generate business from places they wouldn't think of.

Entrepreneurial Veterinarians Are Market Driven

Entrepreneurial veterinarians are *market-driven,* NOT *self-driven.* They deliver what the market wants to buy, not what they want to sell. This is a profound shift in thinking. Many veterinarians choose their practice locations because they prefer the chosen area, without considering whether the market could support another veterinary practice, or at least whether it needed another one the same as all the others.

Maybe veterinarians could get away with this before the recession, but in the New Economy, you must deliver what your market wants or face the consequences.

Entrepreneurial Veterinarians Look Outside for Ideas

We said it before and it bears repeating: if your strategy for success is to copy what every other veterinary practice is doing, then you are doomed to the average results of every other veterinary business. One way entrepreneurial veterinarians make their businesses different is by looking for ideas outside of the veterinary industry.

Here's an example of industrial transplant. Did you know that fast-food drive-thru service was actually an idea taken from banks? Now many other businesses in many other industries have copied the idea. There are drive-thru dry cleaners, drive-thru pharmacies, and even a drive-thru sports book, in (where else?) Las Vegas.

Stop limiting your attention to what's happening inside the veterinary industry, and start looking outside your professional community. What you bring in from beyond your practice and outside the boundaries of veterinary medicine will give you an edge in the New Economy.

CHAPTER 5
THE ULTIMATE QUESTION

In order to be irreplaceable one must always be different.

–Coco Chanel

Now that you've got your head in the right place to make a difference for your veterinary business, let's look at how you can actually do it.

The first step is to ask yourself, what we believe is, *The Ultimate Question* that every veterinary practice owner should be asking themselves every single day:

Why Should a Pet Owner Choose My Veterinary Practice As Opposed To Every Other Option Available To Her?

If the answer for the majority of your clients is either, "You're the closest" OR "You're the cheapest," then your practice could be living on borrowed time!

You see, if you want your practice to thrive in the New Economy then you must have a compelling story, a Unique

Selling Proposition (USP), that will make clients drive past the practice closest to home and pass by the cheapest practice in town to bring their pets to you!

If you don't have that USP (Unique Selling Proposition), then it is only a matter of time before the USP of an existing competitor or a new practice leaves you behind!

Your compelling story, your USP, becomes the focal point of your marketing efforts. It is the talking point that gets you more referrals, the source of pride that makes your employees proud to tell their friends they work at your practice, and the reason why your clients will be happy to travel farther to visit your practice even after you have raised your prices.

You must constantly ask yourself: Why should a pet owner choose my practice rather than any of the other available options, including doing nothing?

Such is the importance of this question that we recommend posting it above your desk and in the non-public areas of your practice—*Why should they choose us?*—as a daily reminder to you and your staff that your clients have other choices, including the choice to do nothing at all. You must give them a good reason to choose you.

If you haven't got a USP, how can you get one?

The good news is that there are lots of ways to develop a USP for your veterinary business. We can suggest a few.

Positioning Your Veterinary Business

A big part of developing your USP is deciding how you will position your practice within your marketplace. By positioning, we mean how you want your veterinary practice to be perceived by your clients and prospective clients, to distinguish it from the other veterinary practices in the market.

Do you want to be regarded as the cheapest vet in town? (We strongly advise against that one.) Do you want to be known for the best in patient care and overall client experience?

Will you try to be all things to all pet owners, or will you specialize in one type of animal (e.g. equine) or one area of veterinary medicine (e.g. dentistry)?

Do you want to be known as the practice that has patients in and out in quick time or the practice known for spending plenty of time with clients and their animals?

If you are uncertain what to position your practice for, a good strategy is to think about what you might position your practice against. For example, if a competing practice in your area is known for its short appointment times and trying to see as many clients as they can within an hour, then you could position your practice against conveyer-belt animal care.

When you position your practice correctly, it should be perceived as the best practice in the area and become the in-demand practice where clients are prepared to wait for an appointment and willing to pay top fees for their pet care.

Ask Your Clients

Another good strategy for developing your USP is to address what your clients like and don't like. To establish that, just ask them!

Ask every client that comes into your practice over the next month what are the top three things they appreciate when taking their pet to a veterinary practice and what are their top three annoyances.

Their answers may not only surprise you but also give you a clue to what your USP might be. For example, if most of your clients list waiting time as a dislike, then figure out how you can give an "On-time, Every Time" guarantee that separates your practice from the crowd. Domino's did very well for a while with free pizzas for late deliveries.

Guarantees

One of the most powerful ways to differentiate yours from other veterinary practices is to offer a money-back guarantee.

Obviously, there are some things you can't guarantee: for instance, you can't always guarantee that the treatment you provide will be successful. There are plenty of other things you can guarantee, though. Start by looking at things that traditionally have caused clients frustration: not being seen at their appointment times, not being informed promptly about the post-procedure status of their pets, or not having their telephone calls returned timely.

Sometimes you can guarantee things that your practice is already doing better than your competition. For example, if you already have protocols in place to return clients' calls within the hour, and your competitors don't, then you might offer this guarantee:

We will return client calls within an hour or your next appointment is free.

Or this:

We will return your call within one hour or take $50 off at your next appointment.

A guarantee like this gives your client peace of mind and reverses their risk. This is very powerful because it raises your standing with your clients and prospective clients as it gives them confidence in your practice. It also sets you apart if your competitors aren't offering guarantees.

The more you can guarantee and the stronger the guarantee you can make, the more attractive your practice will be to prospective clients. It will also seriously alarm your competitors!

Why Do You Buy?

The next time you make a buying decision, whether it's deciding on a restaurant, which car to buy, or even just where to get coffee, ask yourself, "What's their story?"

Why are you choosing them and not the least expensive or most convenient? For example, why do people choose Starbucks over less expensive coffee shops? Why do you travel 20 miles to see your dentist when there are several just around the corner? Your answer will probably have to do with the provider's USP.

If you get your story right, you won't just attract and keep customers, you will create avid fans who will be keen to make referrals, and who will be bringing their pets to you for life!

Once you've answered The Ultimate Question for your veterinary practice, however, you aren't finished. You need to develop strategies to grow your practice in the New Economy. The good news is that we have done the hard work for you and collected in this book the strategies you will need to meet your practice goals.

In the next few chapters, we will discuss that arsenal of practice-growing weapons to make certain that you can become the leading practice in your area. If you adopt these strategies, you will leave your competitors floundering in your wake.

CHAPTER 6
THE THREE PILLARS OF VETERINARY PRACTICE GROWTH

An organization's ability to learn, and translate that learning into action rapidly, is the ultimate competitive advantage.

–Jack Welch

One of our big discoveries has been that all really successful veterinary practices are built on a few core principles, which when systematically applied to any practice, result in sustainable and profitable growth. This research led us to develop **The Three Fundamental and Irrefutable Pillars of Veterinary Practice Growth:**

✓ **Client Attraction** Increase Number of Clients

✓ **Client Retention** Decrease Number of Clients Leaving

✓ **Client Revenue** Increase Value of Each Client

This is a deceptively simple but remarkably powerful framework. We quantify these elements and combine them into a formula that we can apply scientifically in all of our coaching and product development. To see how it works, let's look at an example, simplifying the math for the demonstration.

Suppose a veterinary practice has 2,000 active clients and normally adds 20% new clients each year (i.e. 400) but also loses 15% of existing clients each year (i.e. 300). For the sake of simplicity, let's assume that each client has an annual average value of $300.

This means that the practice's revenue can be calculated roughly as follows:

Revenue = (Existing Customers + New Customers - Lost Customers) x Average Value

Revenue = (2000 + 400 - 300) x $300

Revenue = $630,000

Now let's see what would happen if we improved each factor by a conservative 10 percentage points. This means that there are now 30% more new clients, only 5% are lost, and each client is now worth $330 per year.

Revenue = (2000 + 600 - 100) x $330

Revenue = $825,000

The 10% adjustment of each pillar produced a cumulative effect of 31%, an increase in revenue that clearly demonstrates the power of applying the Three Pillars of Veterinary Practice Growth.

Not only that but, if you applied this 10 percentage point improvement to each Pillar in your practice every year, you would double your practice size is less than three years! This is a goal we encourage our clients to aim for. It's certainly attainable if you systematically apply the strategies in this book.

SECTION 2

CLIENT ATTRACTION

Turning Your Practice into a Pet Owner Magnet:
How to attract more new clients
than you will *ever* need!

CHAPTER 7
THE WHO, THE WHAT, AND THE HOW

Your company's most valuable asset is
how it is known to its customers.

–Brian Tracy

The first (and most obvious) Pillar of Veterinary Practice Growth is to attract more clients. In order to do that there are three questions you must answer:

1. Who is our target market?

2. What is our message to them?

3. How are we going to reach them?

The Who: Determining Your Target Market

It is vital to decide who your ideal client is. If you don't, then you are in danger of casting your net too widely and trying to be all things to all people. Remember that a jack-of-all-trades is master of none.

If you make your veterinary business for everyone, you are essentially making it for no one!

You must think of your target market in much narrower terms than including every pet owner with a pulse because the more you focus your marketing, the more successfully you'll attract clients, the more you can charge them, and the better you can serve them.

In our opinion, there are two segments of the pet-owning community that can be the mainstay of your veterinary business but who have not been targeted by veterinary practices. These are Baby Boomers and affluent pet owners of all generations.

Affluent Pet Owners

How the Affluent Can Bulletproof Your Practice against the Economy

Statistically, people of means are more likely to own pets, so it just makes sense to target them first. Affluent pet owners, whom we define as pet owners with a household income of $100,000 or more, therefore should form a good portion of your client list.

In fact, we would even go so far as to say that there is a direct correlation between the number of affluent clients a practice has and its ability to survive a recession. Why? Because the affluent tend to have more disposable income and are generally the least and last affected by economic downturns.

Think about it: in 2010, even though the average disposable income in the United States was about $250 per month, many individuals and families have actually none; they've been spending more than their income each month. In a society where credit cards have been, until recently, easy to come by, many people have covered their monthly shortfall with plastic.

According to *The Wall Street Journal*, 70 percent of the population of the USA is living paycheck to paycheck. The average US citizen spends $1.26 for every dollar they earn and the average consumer debt for each household is $38,000 and that's not including their mortgage!

The question for you is this: are these the clients you want as the core of your practice? For those with the least disposable income, routine pet care, such as checkups, vaccinations and dental exams, becomes non-essential when the budget is tight. This is not to say that those with the least disposable income love their pets any less, but when it comes to a contest between paying the electricity bill and putting food on the table for their kids (and pets) or paying $50 to their vet for a routine checkup, there is only going to be one winner!

We're not suggesting that you turn people away on the basis of their credit scores. We're suggesting that to bulletproof your practice against economic changes, it makes sense to target clients who are not likely to skip annual appointments or find cost a barrier to your treatment recommendations.

Be the High-End Practice

Do you want to be the veterinary practice of choice for affluent pet owners?

Every profession and industry has its premium product and service providers that cater to the affluent. Why should the veterinary profession be any different? "Birds of a feather flock together." If one veterinary practice in your area is going to have a reputation as the place to be for affluent pet owners, it may as well be yours!

If you're sitting there thinking that there aren't any affluent pet owners in your area, then think again. Every city has affluent neighborhoods and vendors that cater to them (e.g.

Lexus, Mercedes, etc).

We know many veterinary practice owners who worry about their prices and whether their clients can afford them. Please be assured that there are lots of pet owners spending lots of money on their pets. Spending on pets in the USA has increased year after year until it's now estimated at a staggering $47.7 billion![1]

How Affluent Pet Owners Spend Their Money

To show you how freely money is spent for pet care and to demonstrate your potentially billable services, we have given a few examples below. We are not necessarily suggesting that you offer these products or services. We would expect an entrepreneurial veterinarian to be thinking of such things, however, as satellite possibilities to orbit the main veterinary business.

Life Enrichment Services

Life enrichment covers a multitude of services from deep muscle massages to aromatherapy. (When was the last time you had either of those?) They are both offered at LA Dogworks, an upscale pet spa in Hollywood, where the hounds of celebrity owners get star treatment.

These pampered pooches can also get hair color, body wraps, and massages, and the spa even has a hydrotherapy room with heated, filtered water, a scaled-down version of the equipment used for racehorses. The cost for a hydrotherapy, massage, or aromatherapy treatment begins at $75 an hour.

---

[1] Tracy Stapp. "Franchise: Top 10 Trends for 2011. *Enterprise Magazine* (December 2010), p. 123.

Special Diets (Non-medical)

Consumer food trends recently have shown increased awareness of the dangers in highly processed food products. After the recent pet food scare, pet owners are also showing concern about what they put into the bowls of their pets. Organic food for pets has become big business, and the natural pet care market is projected to nearly double by 2012. Affluent pet owners don't seem to mind that gourmet dog foods often cost more per pound than the steaks they order for themselves in gourmet restaurants!

It doesn't stop with food, either. There are companies selling vitamin-enhanced water (www.k9waterco.com) and ionized and alkaline water (realpetwater.com) for pets.

Vitamins

The humanization of pets is fueling consumer demands for products and services that are as good as those available for owners or even better. Vitamin supplements for pets are a multi-million dollar industry (www.onlynaturalpet.com).

Furniture

Pet Furniture is big business and pet furnishings come in every conceivable style: rustic, modern, cottage, eclectic, Victorian, and Mission. There is no reason for Rover's furniture (including bed, nightstand, and armoire) to clash with your decor. In fact, an affluent pet owner is quite happy to spend $399 on a chaise lounge for his dog or $339 on a gold chenille bed (www.pawprintzpetboutique.com). The Tom Claire Co.'s signature bed is a Victorian style creation that comes in various upholstery selections for just $730 (for the bed alone) or $860 (with matching bowl holder)!

Geriatric Care

As dogs and cats get older, hip dysplasia and aching joints are common ailments that affect their mobility. Lots of solutions can now give pets a leg up when they need it. The company Petmate makes non-slip carpeted pet steps ($39.99) at the right height for sofas or beds. The Solvit Products (solvitproducts.com) telescoping ramp (about $150) was designed for SUVs and vans, and some customers have used it in bedrooms, too. Solvit also offers a large HoundAbout Stroller to haul larger dogs. The three-wheel stroller can accommodate pets up to 110 pounds; it has four pockets, a cup holder, and a sunroof, and it costs between $179 and $199.

The Fauna Sauna (faunasauna.com) is a therapeutic heater designed to reduce the pain and stiffness of arthritis or injury. It ranges in price from $75 to $1095.

Green Products

Recyclable products have also entered the pet world.

West Paws Design (westpawdesign.com) offers ecologically friendly dog & cat toys. The cat toys use fabric containing 85% recycled fibers and organic catnip.

Sergeant's Pet Care Products (sergeants.com), in partnership with the National Wildlife Federation, introduced the Protected Wildlife Animal Series plush dog toys that represent various global regions: a green sea turtle (marine life), a polar bear (Arctic life), a jaguar (rainforest) and a bison (North America). Each toy is packaged in recycled materials. A portion of the proceeds goes to the Federation's conservation and education programs.

Wardrobe

Whatever the moral arguments for dressing up your pet, the practical arguments have won. You cannot go anywhere without seeing a dog sporting the latest designer fashions (and some not so fashionable). New York now even hosts a Pet Fashion Week!

Besides the big designer brands such as Burberry® (Dog Coats for $211) and Louis Vuitton®, there are thousands of smaller companies in what is now a multi-billion dollar industry. Companies such as Little Lily, a six-year-old company that clears over $1 million a year, sell products that include doggie slippers, bikinis, and even canine versions of Oscar-night gowns.

Of course, that's not forgetting the designer collars and even jewelry that are now available for the discerning pet.

It would seem that walking is beneath the affluent small dog, as there is also a booming market in designer bags in which these little dogs can ride, and even strollers are available, specifically for driving pampered pets.

Pet Grooming

Pet Grooming is another booming industry, with mobile grooming ever more popular. The affluent pet owner can obtain full service which, with extras, can cost hundreds of dollars (see http://www.stylenpaws.com). For baths at home there are thousands of shampoos and conditioners that are often more expensive than the human equivalent.

Luxury Pet Products

There is virtually nothing you can think of that you can't purchase for your pet. Visit www.PetGadgets.com to find everything from a blow dryer ($99.95 + Shipping) to the Soft Heart Pillow ($110.00), which is embroidered with your pet's name and holds its cremated remains! And what discerning dog could do without its Wowo Curved Wood Single Bowl Raised

Feeder($106 to $166) from www.thesharperdog.com.

Behavioral Specialists

TV programs such as *The Dog Whisperer*, with dog behavioral specialist Cesar Millan, and *It's Me Or The Dog*, with Victoria Stilwell, have seen a growth in demand for canine behavioral services. Canine Psychology Centers are starting to pop up around the U.S., and affluent owners are lining up for their services.

Dog Waste Removal

The growing willingness of owners to spare no expense for their animals has also made outsourcing of the yucky aspects of pet care a burgeoning business. More than 350 service agencies, with onomatopoetic names such as Doody Duty, Scoopy-Poo, and Pooper Trooper, have sprung up solely to relieve owners of the need even to pick up a pet's waste. There are even some services that will see to emptying your cat's litter tray.

Posthumous Pet Care

According to The American Pet Products Association's 2009-2010 National Pet Owners Survey, 7% of pet owners have made financial provisions for pets in their will, although other surveys suggest that this figure is nearer 27%.

Grief Counselors

Well-loved pets become part of the family, so when pets die the family can experience trauma. For affluent pet owners, there are animal grief counselors to help cope with the demise of beloved pets.

You will be well aware of the pain pet owners experience when they lose what to them was a family member, especially if they have no children at home, as in the case of the empty nesters. Some older persons living alone face the loss of a pet as the loss of protection and the onset of profound loneliness. It should come as no surprise that those who can afford it are likely to seek counseling.

Dog Walking

Professional people quite often do not have the time to exercise their dogs properly, and for people with disabilities exercise is sometimes just not an option. Consequently, professional dog walking services have sprouted up all over the country.

Dog Sitting

For the affluent pet owner who vacations at least once, and more likely several times, a year or for professionals who are out all day, dog sitting services are available so that someone comes into the home to provide care and companionship for their pets.

Pet Photography & Portraits

Now that pets are fully fledged members of the family, it is quite as common to see a photo or portrait of a pet on the wall as it is any human family member. It's not inexpensive either; check out www.petwhisperart.com where a pet portrait (made from a photo) starts at $159.00.

Luxury Boarding

We've left the best until last. We suspect that many of you will be thinking, "Well, these items may be being purchased in Beverley Hills or Manhattan but not in our backyard." We can assure you that these purchases are happening all over the country.

To prove our point we'd like to introduce you to the Barkley Pet Hotel & Day Spa based in Cleveland, Ohio. Yes, that's the same Cleveland, Ohio, that is often ranked as "THE poorest big city in America," and with the greatest of respect to the people of Cleveland, not widely regarded as an amenity-rich area.

Yet it is home to one of the most exclusive pet hotels in the country. The Barkley is a $4.5 million dollar pet paradise spread over 3-acres of urban real estate. The goal of this hotel is to rank among the best pet care facilities. A true pet hotel, not kennel, offering 5-star guest services that include clean, high-quality bedding, daily maid and linen service, continuous fresh water, multiple daily walks and feedings, soothing music, customized climate control, and plenty of TLC.

The Barkley is home to a one-of-a-kind Health & Wellness Center that offers a variety of services provided by experienced in-house licensed veterinarians. These services include laser therapy, joint mobilization, acupuncture, canine hydrotherapy, weight management programs, and thermal therapy.

The Barkley is usually booked solid and in 2010 opened a second Hotel in Westlake Village, California, near Los Angeles.

Be very clear: affluent pet owners have money to spend on their pets and they are willing to spend it, especially those in the category of pet parents where their pet plays the role of their child.

Now that we've convinced you that a large proportion of affluent clients is a good thing, let's see where you can find them.

Finding the Affluent Pet Owners

There are two easy ways to identify affluent pet owners in

your area.

The scientific approach is to use a list broker. A list broker will rent a mailing list that matches stated criteria. Did you know, for example, that is possible to rent a list of affluent pet owners within the zip codes surrounding your practice?

A quick Google® search will present you with many list brokers, so it's best to speak to two or three before you decide to rent a list. Ask how often the list is updated and whether the addresses have been verified. Once you have rented a list, cross reference it with your own client list, so that you don't send out your new-client offers to current clients.

A second way to find affluent pet owners is not very scientific at all but still very effective. Ask your local realtor where the affluent neighborhoods are in your area; you can be sure that these will be a good source of affluent pet owners for your practice. Statistics show that 67% of Americans own pets and, as we said earlier, this figure is higher for affluent people. You can expect 3 out of 4 affluent homes to include a pet.

If you rent your list it will be easy to make your message personal because you have the pet owners' names. You can also individualize your message by neighborhood, however, if you have can find a recent city directory. Can you think of other ways to gain access to groups of affluent pet owners?

There is no doubt in our mind that having a significant percentage of affluent pet owners in your practice will make your practice virtually recession proof and allow quicker and more sustained growth. It is relatively easy to find out where the affluent pet owners live, so making a conscious and concerted effort to attract them should be high on your list of priorities.

If you don't make an effort to attract affluent pet owners,

then it is only a matter of time before your competitors beat you to it. (Perhaps they are even reading this book right now!) Take the initiative and claim the position of high-end vet for your marketing area before it's too late.

Baby Boomer Pet Owners

The other target market that veterinary practices should select for priority attention is Baby Boomer pet owners. Baby Boomers are defined by the United States Census Bureau as persons born during the demographic birth boom between 1946 and 1964. They make up roughly one-third of the U.S. population.

There are 78 million baby boomers in the U.S., currently accounting for 28% of the population. Combine this with the fact that baby boomers own more than 77% of the nation's financial assets, and you can see why they are a market you can't afford to ignore but should seek out and nurture.

"Baby boomers are keeping their pets longer and are willing to do $5,000 surgeries on them, there are even denture products to help keep their teeth longer." says Bob Vetere, president of the American Pet Products Manufacturers Association.

While Baby Boomers tend to have more disposable income than their younger compatriots, e.g., their mortgages will be paid off in many cases and they may have savings, they share a characteristic of even greater significance to your veterinary practice.

Empty Nesters Make Ideal Clients

Many of the Baby Boomers are "empty nesters." Their kids have left home, and they have filled the emptiness with a pet.

In her book *Turning Silver Into Gold: How to Profit in the New Boomer Marketplace*, baby boomer expert Mary Furlong claims that nearly 40 percent of persons between the ages of 55 and 64 own a pet. She confirms that "empty nesters treat their pets like children, with equal privileges and care." Even the Beverly Hills Hilton is pet-friendly, she says, "and the family retriever now has his own raincoat."

Baby Boomers are at an age where their children have grown up and left the family home. Add to this a growing trend for families to move farther away from their hometowns in search of employment, meaning fewer opportunities to spoil the grandchildren, and it's easy to see why pets are considered by many as the new children and grandchildren.

The good news for veterinary practices is that Boomers are fairly easy to identify. Just as with affluent pet owners, it is possible to rent a list of pet owners within your area within a certain age range. The main difference in marketing to Baby Boomers is that the language used in your marketing messages should be tailored to resonate with their demographic.

Establish your credibility with honest testimonials, verifiable facts, and accurate descriptions of what your practice offers, and you'll have the ear of the Boomer consumer. Intelligent, optimistic, and full of idealism, the Baby Boomer appreciates images that reflect how they see themselves and the times in which they grew up. They expect marketing messages to be consistent with their values and motivations.

The Silver Surfers

Baby boomers are also easily found online; over 64% of those aged 50–64 use the Internet. For example, at the end of 2010, there were 40,520,240 American Baby Boomers using Facebook. We know they don't all own pets, and they don't all live in your marketing area, but a good percentage will. In addition, as you will see later, Facebook will allow you to narrow your search specifically to find Boomers with an interest in dogs or cats. So a direct-response Facebook ad targeting Baby Boomer dog owners could be very fruitful.

The What: Your Marketing Message

Once you have decided who your market is, you have to decide what message you are going to deliver. There are two things to bear in mind when crafting your marketing message—tone and content.

First, the underlying tone of your marketing messages should be based on your USP, how you are positioning yourself in the market. That's not to say you will deliver the same message every time, just that you will consistently highlight what makes you special.

Second, you should tailor your individual messages to convey an offer that is appropriate for the services or products you are promoting and for the audiences you are sending them to. The more tailored your message is to your target audience, the more impact it will have. This means it is necessary not only that your messages for prospective clients must be different from those for existing clients but also that you must have different messages for the different niches and sub-niches you are targeting.

For example, the message you craft for a campaign to attract affluent pet owners should be different from the message you craft to attract baby boomer pet owners. You may even want to take this a stage further by creating different campaigns for different subsets (or sub-niches) of your market.

In the case of the affluent pet owners you may want to vary your message depending on their specific household income. A pet owner making $250,000+ per year may lead a different lifestyle from that of someone in the $100,000 to $150,000 per year category. Alternatively, you may want to craft your message to a specific neighborhood, especially if there is some prestige associated with living there.

In the case of Baby Boomer pet owners, you may craft one message to those between the ages of 46 and 55, who grew up in an era which introduced punk rock and had the Cold War as a backdrop, and a slightly different one to those between the ages of 56 and 64, who grew up with The Beatles, Jimi Hendrix, and the backdrop of Vietnam. Alternatively you might want to send a different message to female recipients from the one you send to male recipients. And you may want to alter their messages according to income levels.

As a general rule of thumb, the more specific you make your message to your audience, the more power and impact it will have.

One of the most important things to consider in your marketing is the language you use: make sure it is tailored to the intended recipients. For example, the language and offer you have for affluent pet owners may be different from that for Baby Boomer pet owners. Your message to affluent pet owners might try to convey the prestige of being a member of your practice while a message to Baby Boomers might be more nostalgic, reminding them of a time when your veterinarian knew you by name and was a friend of the family.

The key point is that you want to be different from all of the veterinary practices out there. You do not want to deliver the same message to everyone you reach with your marketing. By tailoring your message to your market and to the sub-niches within your market, you will differentiate yourself from your competitors who target all prospective clients in the same way.

Your clients and prospective clients will appreciate your

efforts and identify with your practice as the place for them and their pets.

The How: Delivering Your Message

With your target market in sight and your message clearly defined, now you need to decide on the best way to deliver your message to your market. There are dozens of media choices to consider, including direct mail, newspaper, magazines, Internet, radio, and TV. Make sure you choose the ones best suited to your audience.

In this age of big businesses spending millions on their marketing, it's difficult to compete for the attention of desirable potential clients. A study by Texas A&M University estimated that the average American is subjected to 850 commercial advertisements every day. Other studies suggest that this may be conservative, that the real level of exposure could be well over 1,000 ads per day. These statistics strike fear into any small-business owner who is hoping to connect with the public through advertising.

So how can your veterinary practice punch through this clutter to communicate a message and acquire clients?

Many vets make the mistake of modeling their advertising on that of big business. They end up spending (i.e., wasting) money on image, brand, and presence. The big companies have a myriad of different reasons for the way they spend their vast marketing budgets, and most have little to do with getting clients and making sales.

In contrast, we realize that the average veterinary practice doesn't have the luxury of doing Coca-Cola® style brand-building advertising. Vets need a quick return (measured in days not years). This is why we encourage our clients to use Direct Response Marketing techniques.

CHAPTER 8
DIRECT RESPONSE MARKETING

The key is not to call the decision maker.
The key is to have the decision maker call you.

–Jeffrey Gitomer

What Is Direct Response Marketing?

Direct response marketing is an approach to marketing that aims to elicit an immediate, measurable response from the prospective client. In some cases the immediate response is an actual sale, while in other cases it is moving the prospective client down the sales funnel.

Direct response marketing offers a very different approach from the style of marketing you see in most magazines and on TV, created by the big Madison Avenue advertising agencies. For instance, direct response marketing has the following characteristics that you will very rarely see in big agency advertising.

1. A Response Is Always Sought

   In direct response marketing, the recipient is given a reason to respond, is given clear instructions on how to respond, and is specifically asked to respond (a call to action).

2. Long Compelling Sales Copy

   Direct response marketing in known for providing as much benefit-laden copy as is needed to convince the recipient to respond. Long copy has been proven to work better than short copy in sales letters.

3. Irresistible Offer

   In order to get the reader/listener/viewer to respond, the direct response ad makes an irresistible offer. This is not necessarily a cheap or discounted offer. An irresistible offer is simply a compelling reason for the prospect to respond. This could be something as simple as a free report containing some information of value, or it could be something more substantial, such as premium gift for actually taking action to make an appointment.

4. Multi-step, Multimedia

   Where direct response marketing really differs from traditional forms of marketing is that there is never just one step and the direct response marketing campaign usually involves multiple forms of media.

   For example, step one might be newspaper advertising, step two a follow-up letter to those who responded to the newspaper ad, and step three a telephone call. Alternatively, the first step could be a letter and the second an e-mail. The point is that there are multiple steps and each one can be carried out using a wide choice of media.

5. Measurable Results

A very important characteristic of direct response marketing is that the response can be measured. Direct response marketers know that if they spend $X on a campaign they should get $Y back, because they have tracked the results of previous similar campaigns.

Figure 1 shows the direct response marketing funnel as it could be applied to your veterinary practice.

Permission Based Marketing

As you can see from the diagram, the first step in the sales funnel is to generate leads rather than actually to make an appointment or sale. There are two reasons for this.

First, it removes sales pressure so that your marketing can be about helping and educating your prospects rather than trying to sell to them.

Second, there are pet owners or soon-to-be pet owners who do not need your services right now but may be interested in using them in the future. This gives them the opportunity to connect with you irrespective of current need.

In most cases you just want the prospective client to raise a hand and say, "Yes, I'm a potential client," giving you permission to start recruitment. This is sometimes referred to as permission-based marketing. In other words, your potential clients have acknowledged that they may be interested in what you have to offer, and your marketing message becomes something that they look forward to (which dramatically increases its effectiveness), instead of an unwelcome intrusion.

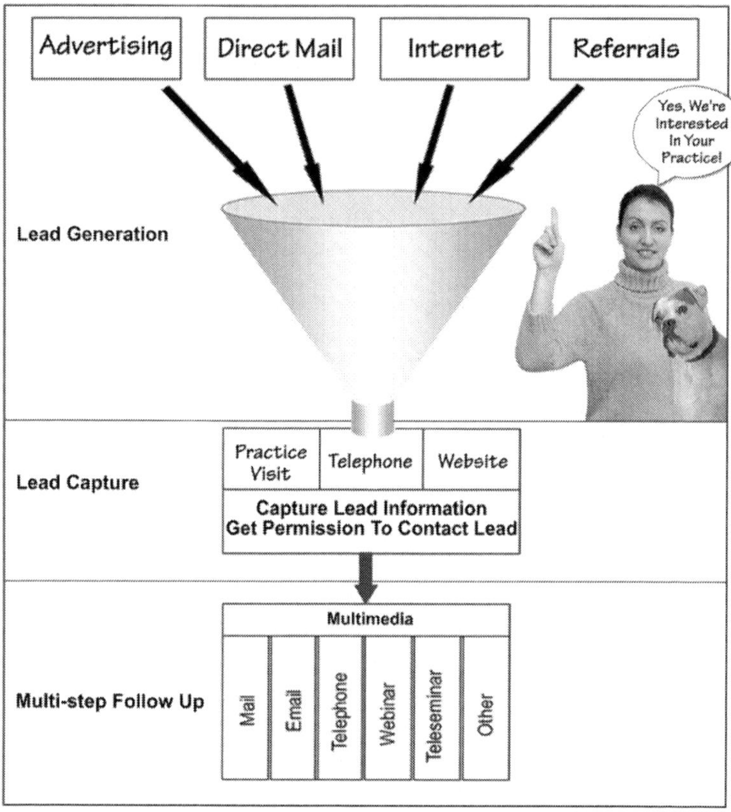

Figure 1 – Direct Response Marketing Funnel

It is easier and more effective to make offers to a list of prospective clients who have already shown an interest in what you do than it is to make offers to a "cold" list of unknown persons who may or may not even be pet owners.

With the sales funnel, you use lots of different methods to get pet owners to "raise their hands:" ads in newspapers, local magazines, and Yellow Pages; direct mail; Internet marketing;

and referral programs.

You get prospects to raise their hands by making a compelling offer to any who visit your practice, give you a call, or visit your Website.

As soon as a hand is raised, you want to move the process through the funnel, capturing contact details and getting permission to send more information. Your prospect usually will be happy to provide contact details in exchange for the information or gift you offered as part of your lead generation in stage one.

With contact details safely in hand, you can now move on to stage three and continue marketing until the prospect either becomes a client or tells you to stop. It is in stage three that your goal is to turn the prospective client into an actual client. To accomplish this, you might call, send letters or e-mails, or offer an invitation to a free seminar, live in your practice, on the telephone, or over the Internet.

In case this is starting to set off alarm bells in your head, remember that you have permission; everything you send or offer in stage three should be in the category of "welcome guest" rather than "unwelcome pest." You want to nurture the prospects on your list; you most certainly do not want to offend them. So every time you contact a prospect in this stage, you will be sending either a compelling offer or valuable information that is clearly beneficial.

This approach has been proven effective for growing a small business's client base. (It's effective in virtually all small businesses, not just veterinary practices.) It is flexible and can be applied in almost any situation, using whatever advertising media are available, affordable, and acceptable to your prospect population.

Internal Marketing & External Marketing

Internal marketing and external marketing are terms often heard in relation to practice-based businesses and other businesses that work with a client base.

External marketing is the term used for marketing to prospective clients. Internal marketing is marketing to your current clients.

Although this part of the book is about attracting new clients—external marketing—it is important to point out that direct response marketing is not aimed solely at new clients. Many of the direct response marketing strategies explored here can and should be used with current clients. For example, the chapter on referrals involves marketing to current clients in order to get them to refer new ones.

Multi-step marketing campaigns are ideal for use with existing clients to promote preventative medicine programs such as dental hygiene and weight loss. These campaigns are also appropriate for renewing contact with clients who have missed annual appointments.

Some other internal marketing strategies are presented in the sections on Client Retention and Client Revenue.

In the following chapters we will show you some of the ways we coach our Veterinary Practice Profits clients to implement these strategies for the profit of their own veterinary businesses.

CHAPTER 9
ADVERTISING DONE THE RIGHT WAY

There is no need for advertisements to look like advertisements. If you make them look like editorial pages, you will attract about 50 per cent more readers.

–David Ogilvy (Advertising Legend)

Although many advertising principles are applicable to Internet marketing, in this chapter we will focus on offline advertising, such as local newspapers, local magazines, Yellow Pages, local radio, local TV, and anywhere else you can place an ad without using prospects' contact information.

It has been our experience that veterinarians struggle to make display ads work in newspapers and local magazines. So let's review the main keys to running winning ads. By winning ads, we mean those that attract prospects and provide a return on your investment. Here's how to do it.

Pick the Right Media

Be sure to choose the right media outlet. For example, if you are doing a newspaper ad to target pet owners within a specific geographic area or within a certain part of town or within a small radius around your practice, then you would do better to advertise in the weekly local paper for that area rather than the daily city paper. The local is more targeted, and will be cheaper too.

Local "Lifestyle" magazines and shoppers (yes, those throwaways) could also be a good place for direct response ads, and many locales have independent mini business directories that are delivered monthly to selected homes within their catchment areas.

Negotiate Terms

All media outlets have a rate card that states their prices for advertising once or several times. These rates are almost always negotiable. So negotiate the rate.

Never commit to a long term contract. You want to be able to measure the results of running the ad before you consider further advertising in the publication. For example, while sometimes a poor response to an ad is because the ad itself is weak, sometimes it's because the publication you have chosen is not the right one for your intended market. Therefore, you would not want to have signed a long-term contract only to discover that the publication is not going to work out for you.

Use Direct Response Techniques, Not Branding

This is probably the most important point. Most ads you see in newspapers, magazines, and Yellow Pages are brand-building ads. They have the company name emblazoned across the top, they give contact details, and they list the company's products or services. They may also include a graphic and the company logo.

We call these type of ads "tombstone" ads because they provide about as much information as a tombstone does and are equally appealing to prospective clients! Figure 2 shows an example of a brand-building ad or "tombstone."

If you look through the veterinary section in your local Yellow Pages or in one of the many local ad magazines or in your local newspaper, this is the type of ad you are likely to see. To be fair to veterinary practices, the style of this ad is typical of almost every other business too.

XYZ Veterinary Clinic
"Somewhere Special
For You & Your Pet"
• High Quality Care For Your Pets
• Open 6 Days • Emergencies Taken
• Spays/Neuters • Dogs, Cats, Rabbits
3456 Miami Lake Dr. Orlando
Tel: (345) 567-8910
www.xyzveterinary.com

Figure 2 - A Typical "Tombstone" Veterinary Ad

As you can see, this ad doesn't give the pet owner any reason to choose this practice over any other. After all, doesn't every veterinary practice claim to provide high quality care and perform spays and neuters? It would be a pretty poor veterinary practice if it didn't; a prospective client wouldn't expect anything less than what this one advertises.

The only part of this ad that might actually persuade a pet owner to choose it is the address, but only if that pet owner lived in the very near vicinity or on the same street! In that case, chances are that the prospect would already know you existed, so ultimately this ad is a complete waste of time and money.

In contrast, a direct response ad does not look like an ad! If you are advertising in a newspaper or magazine, the best type of ad is an advertorial, which is designed to look like the content of the publication. Whether you are doing a full-page or half-page advertorial or a smaller Yellow Pages type ad it MUST have the following components:

A Good Headline

You must have a hook to make your prospective client stop and think, *This could matter to me.*

An Irresistible Offer

Prospective clients need to know what's in it for them. You have to give them a reason to call, go to your Website, or visit your practice.

A Deadline or Scarcity Warning

Once you have gotten them to read your ad, and you have offered them something they want, you need to make sure prospects are not going to procrastinate. If they put your ad down without taking action, you've probably lost them.

One way to get them to act now is to give them a deadline or tell them that your offer is limited to a certain number of people.

A Call to Action

Finally, you need to give clear instructions about what to do next. If you don't tell your prospect how to respond, or if you make the instructions too complicated, then you may lose a client. There's a saying that "a confused buyer never buys." Yes, and a confused ad reader never responds!

There are other components that may increase response, such as testimonials, which we'll discuss later, but these four components MUST be in every ad you publish if you want a return on your investment.

Remember: the purpose of advertising is to get prospects to pick up the phone, go to your Website, or visit your practice, so that they become clients at a cost that is both measurable and profitable to your veterinary business.

Now you know the key components of a direct response ad and why you should be using them for the benefit of your practice. Next you need to know what a direct response ad actually looks like.

Well, if you subscribe to any golf magazines, you already will have seen direct response ads. They are used regularly to sell all manner of golf-related products and services. Direct response ads are not just for golf, though; they can be found in almost any popular magazine.

You know direct response ads work, because advertising in these kinds of magazines is very expensive, and yet you see the same ads appearing week after week and month after month. This is a sure sign that the ad is profitable for the advertiser.

Just so that you are not in any doubt, however, let's analyze a great example of a direct response ad for a veterinary practice. The ad in the figure 3 is aimed at parents who are shopping for

Christmas.

"WARNING! Parents: Are You Buying A Puppy For Your Child This Christmas? FREE Classes Reveal How To Ensure This Isn't A Decision You Will Come To Regret!"

If you are a parent who intends to make your child's dreams come true this Christmas with the addition of a new puppy to your household then this could be the most important message you will ever read!

Every Christmas, parents across the country delight their children with a new puppy but for far too many this delight often turns into traumatic disappointment and broken hearted kids.

You see, what parents don't realize is that buying a puppy is a major life changing event. In fact it is common for these same parents to buy puppies for Christmas only to attempt to re-home them come January, just as soon as the novelty has worn off.

When reality sets in and as you realize that you now have another "child" to deal with… one which is making a mess all over your carpet and behaving in an unruly manner… the first reaction is often one of panic and an immediate search for a new home for the pet.

If you would like to avoid the stress of housing a new puppy, at what is traditionally a hectic time of year, then don't worry as help is at hand.

FREE Puppy Preparation classes are now available in your area to ensure that the arrival of your new puppy doesn't end in tears!

In these classes you will discover:

- **The 3 questions you must ask when buying a puppy** (the answers to these could save you hundreds of dollars!)
- **How to prepare for your new arrival** (knowing this will save you and your puppy a lot of unnecessary stress!)
- **The key symptoms you MUST look out for that are critical to your puppies health and survival in his first few days at home** (not knowing these can have grave consequences for your pet!)
- **The easy to use training tips that will ensure your puppy learns quickly** (you and your carpets will be thankful you found these!)
- **Much more...**

To reserve a FREE place in one of our classes just call XYZ Veterinary Clinic on (345) 567-8910. Places are limited so call now to avoid disappointment.

As veterinarians it is our duty to look out for the well being of puppies so please do the right thing and make sure you give your new puppy the best start in life he can get. **Remember a dog is for life not just for Christmas.**

Figure 3 - Direct Response Advert Example

As you can see, it looks nothing like a typical ad but more like an article. Notice also that it includes the four key components plus the extra bullet points designed to convey the main benefits of our offer, in this case Free Puppy Preparation classes. The object is recruitment to a free class at your practice—a good thing for you, the family, and the puppy.

Do you think parents who answered this ad would be good prospects to become clients of your practice? Of course they would!

This ad would be ideal for a local newspaper or a local community magazine. If you lived near a big city and you knew some other veterinary practices in non-competing areas around the same city, you could team up with them and share the cost of advertising in the daily city paper. You would just need to adjust the ad to say "To reserve a FREE place, call the veterinary clinic listed below that is most convenient for you." You would then list each practice name with its area code and telephone number.

The aim of this ad is to get soon-to-be puppy owners into your practice, where you will have the opportunity to offer them puppy starter kits and sign them up as long-term clients. Note that in your ad you're not asking them to become clients; there is no sales pressure. You are offering them something valuable, completely free, and of great interest to them.

Make Your Ad about Something

Our direct response ad example is for a very specific offer at a very specific time of year. This is profoundly different from the tombstone ad we showed earlier, which is the sort of ad that runs all year round. It is also from a different strategy of two-step appointment generation.

Being About What Your Clients Are Thinking

There is a saying in marketing that "you should enter the conversation in your prospect's mind." In our direct response ad example, we are attempting to enter a conversation that many parents have (or should have!) before Christmas when they contemplate buying a puppy for their child.

At other times of year, you could use the same offer but make it about buying a puppy for the child's birthday or for Easter. You could also connect an offer either directly or indirectly with other events such as the New Year, Fourth of July, Halloween, Thanksgiving, or Hanukkah. Pet management often becomes a family problem when school starts, so the ad could be effective at the end of summer.

A similar approach can target a narrower audience with a specific problem. For example, you could have an ad with this headline:

**WARNING: Does Your Dog Have Bad Breath?
This May Be a Sign of Something More Sinister!
Discover How a Simple Check Could Save Your Pet
...and Put Your Mind at Ease!**

You could then describe the potential problems associated with dental disease and offer a dental check-up.

Two-Step Appointment Generation

With the previous approach you are trying to sell your service directly, but as we explained earlier, another approach is a two-step process that generate leads first and then converts "hot" prospects to sales or appointments. In the dental example, you might use the following headline to achieve this.

**WARNING: Does Your Dog Have Bad Breath?
He Could Be in Danger! FREE Report Reveals the
Critical Signs You MUST Look For!**

You could then explain that while dogs are not known for having sweet-smelling breath, they shouldn't have foul-smelling breath either! You could describe some of the real and present dangers associated with bad breath and offer a free report on the causes of bad breath and the symptoms associated with those.

While this type of ad will not result in immediate appointments, it should have a better response than the previous ad and result in lots of qualified leads, because you are not asking for commitment to an actual appointment. In other words, lots of pet owners will raise their hands to say *Yes, my dog's breath does smell bad, tell me more.* The importance of this should not be underestimated; now you can not only write or e-mail these prospects about your dental offer, but knowing they are concerned pet owners, you can send them other offers too!

The Yellow Pages Exception

Yellow Pages used to be the mainstay of any small business marketing activities. In our opinion, the advent of the Internet has meant that it is no longer as effective as it once was. According to a report by the Pew Research Center's Internet & American Life Project in May 2010, 79% of Americans over 18 used the Internet. With access to the Internet growing every day, there may even come a time in the not too distant future when the Yellow Pages becomes obsolete.

While it is still around, however, there are two types of pet owner that use the Yellow Pages, making Yellow Pages an advertising medium that veterinary practices should still seriously consider.

Pet Owners over the Age of 50

It is widely accepted that the younger generation, who have been brought up using computers and now the Internet, will generally use the Internet, whether it be on a computer or their Internet-enabled cell phones, to find local businesses, including veterinary practices.

While the over-50s are learning their way around the Internet at an ever growing rate, many still prefer the Yellow Pages and find them quicker to use when searching for local businesses. Like reading books, for some people nothing beats flipping through paper pages.

Pet Owners with an Emergency

Businesses who provide solutions to household emergencies, such as plumbers and air conditioning service companies, usually do well from Yellow Pages advertising. If you provide emergency pet care, then you too could profit from advertising in the Yellow Pages.

Obviously, Yellow Pages advertising differs from display advertising in that you have to keep the same ad for the entire year, so it has to reflect your USP rather than any specific seasonal offer. Our direct response principles still stand, though, and they are even more important in the Yellow Pages, where all ads generally look the same and you need a way to stand out.

One of the reasons your prospects price shop is because they look through the Yellow Pages and find that all the ads for veterinarians are saying and offering the same things. They all offer "affordable convenient care," they all say that "new patients are welcome,'" and—surprise! surprise!— they all offer spays, neuters, and vaccines!

Because all the ads offer the same thing, prospective clients have no choice but to conclude that veterinary services are a commodity. As you know, when something is perceived as a commodity, consumers will shop for the lowest price, so pet owners are reduced to phoning all the veterinary practices close to them to find the cheapest one.

Of course, advertising in the Yellow Pages is not cheap, so

you cannot afford to gamble on your ad being seen or that you will be distinguished from other veterinary practices.

How do you make your Yellow Pages ad a sure thing?

First, be warned that your Yellow Pages sales representative will not like the style of ad you are going to request. He or she will try to convince you that it is ugly, that there is too much copy, and that it won't work because it doesn't look like all the other ads. But these are the very reasons why you want it, why it will work, and why you will make all the other ads irrelevant to your prospective clients!

Remember, Yellow Pages representatives are sales persons, not marketing experts. If your rep tells you that your ad isn't going to work, then you've probably done it right! In fact, we know of one rogue Yellow Pages rep who discovered direct response marketing techniques for himself and started advising his clients to use them. Not surprisingly, his clients started getting a much better response from their ads. As a result, they went from seeing the Yellow Pages as a necessary evil to seeing it as an essential marketing tool. Sadly, most Yellow Pages reps aren't so resourceful; they're just interested in selling tombstone ads because that's all they know or want to know.

David Ogilvy, often called The Father of Advertising, is widely credited with coining the phrase, "The more you tell, the more you sell." This applies to your Yellow Pages ad.

Figure 4 shows a sample direct response full-page Yellow Pages ad. This is an ad for a practice positioned against the least expensive veterinary practices who offer shorter appointments.

You can see that it has a compelling headline, a compelling offer ($25 gift card for new clients), and a call to action. Obviously, because Yellow Pages ads appear all year long, it is difficult to use a deadline or scarcity warning, so in order to create some urgency, the ad uses the statement, "Don't Gamble With Your Pet's Life."

The ad is further enhanced with some testimonials from satisfied clients, a pet-care hotline that promotes even more benefits of your practice, and a money-back guarantee. Your photo should also be in the ad, because "people buy people," and a photo helps you create a rapport with the your client before you have even met.

We recommend using a photo of yourself dressed in your veterinary uniform, smiling, and holding a small dog or cat. The uniform conveys your authority and expertise as a veterinarian, your smile conveys friendliness, and holding the dog or cat conveys caring for animals. A picture conveys a thousand words or, in this case, three characteristics we now don't have to write copy and find space for

An alternative for this type of full-page ad would be to do it in advertorial style the same as you would for a newspaper or magazine. The point is that your ad will be different from all the other veterinary ads in the Yellow Pages, and it is your ad that will get attention.

Figure 4 - Sample Full Page Yellow Pages Ad

Our next Yellow Pages ad (see figure 5) is a perfect example of a smaller ad that will definitely not be popular with your Yellow Pages representative. It will be popular with prospective clients, however, and it will be different from any other veterinary ad in the directory.

"How To Choose A Veterinarian"

If you are looking for a Veterinarian for your pet but aren't sure which one to choose, don't worry help is at hand. As a free service to readers of this directory you can now call a **Free Recorded Message** that reveals:

How to choose a Veterinary Practice that will have your pets best interests at heart and the 10 Things Your Veterinarian MUST Recommend, Perform and Believe In.

To discover this important information just call 1-800-XXX-XXXX, 24 hours a day, 7 days a week and listen to the free recorded message. Alternatively, if you would prefer to speak to a veterinary expert just call (XXX) XXX-XXXX for a free telephone consultation Monday to Friday 9AM to 5PM.

Figure 5 - Smaller Yellow Pages Ad

The reason this ad will work so well is that it doesn't look like an ad. It actually looks like a notice the Yellow Pages have put in to help you choose a veterinarian! To make this ad work, you need to provide a recorded message (this is actually very easy and inexpensive to set up) that gives some great tips on how to choose a veterinary practice. Of course, the tips should include all the benefits of using your practice, and the message should include ten things you recommend, perform, and believe in! You must also provide an alternative number that readers can call to speak to a live person. Again, it is easy to set up a number which calls a phone in your practice.

Your veterinary expert can be anyone in your practice who is qualified to give out the information a pet owner needs to consider in choosing a practice. If the caller wants actual veterinary medical advice, however, then schedule a visit to your practice to see a DVM.

CHAPTER 10
DIRECT MAIL

The formula for business success is simple: Find out what people want and give it to them. But you must find out what they really want not just what they say they want.

–Gary Halbert (Direct Mail and Copywriting Legend)

Direct mail is probably the most powerful weapon in your marketing arsenal because, while not all of your clients will have a computer or buy the newspaper you advertise in, they will all have a mail box! And what is one of the very first things you do when you return home from your practice? Open your mail, of course!

We define direct mail as a multi-step sequence of direct response mail pieces sent directly to prospective (or current) clients at their mailing addresses. The address list you use has been generated from your previous marketing efforts (for example, a direct response ad in the local newspaper), has been extracted from your veterinary practice management system (in the case of internal marketing), or has been purchased from a list broker.

(Remember, you can buy lists affluent pet owners in your area and even lists of affluent pet owners born between 1946 and 1964, Baby Boomers.)

Like any other advertising, the sole objective of the direct-mail piece is to elicit a response—either a request for more information or a visit to your practice. There are many different types of direct mail, but each must overcome three hurdles before the recipient can even think about responding to you.

1. Your mail must be delivered.

   Despite some horror stories of postal workers dumping large quantities of mail rather than delivering them, the U. S. Postal Service is still pretty reliable. Your main concern is to make sure that your mailing list contains valid addresses. If you have bought your list from a list broker, make sure it was run against the National Change of Address (NCOA) database to ensure valid content. If you are using a professional printer to prepare your mail, then they should also be able to provide this service.

2. Your mail must be opened.

   Assuming your mail has been delivered to a good address, the next obstacle in your path is to get it opened (postcards excluded). Good Housekeeping Magazine did a survey asking the first thing people do when they get home from work. The good news they found is that most Americans open their mail first! The bad news was that they open it over their trash cans!

   When sending mail to prospects, there are two

strategies you can use to ensure that your mail gets opened. First, send your mail in plain white envelopes with live stamps and a handwritten address. Second, consider using 3D (lumpy) mail. Lumpy mail is a term often used to describe mail that contains an object that turns your flat two-dimensional mail piece into a lumpy three-dimensional mail piece.

Lumpy mail works because it has to be on top of the pile in the mailbox and because the recipient is compelled to open it out of curiosity to see what is inside. Typically, the enclosed object will be tied in with the headline and theme of the mailing. For example, a letter to reactivate clients who have missed their annual checkup might include a small plastic boomerang with a "We want you back" headline. The 3D objects usually cost very little to purchase (see the Resources section for details).

Tip: It has been proven that you can further increase your open rate by using stamps with a design, rather than standard stamps, and by using multiple stamps, rather than just one.

3. Your mail must be read.

Now that your recipient has opened your mail, the real work begins. You need to grab attention and get that piece of mail read. The hook is a compelling headline. It should shout out that this mailing is a must-read and the recipient will be missing out by failing to read it.

Our three favorite methods of direct mail are:

1. Letters

2. Postcards

3. Tear sheets

1. Letters

Letters are powerful. They allow you to say as much as you need to say to convey your story. Like your other advertising pieces (hint: do not use letterhead stationery), they should have a compelling headline, an irresistible offer, a deadline or scarcity warning, and a call to action, all wrapped in the story.

Don't be afraid to make your letter as long as is necessary to educate readers about why they should bring their pets to your practice. Despite what you might think, or what you may have heard, the longer the letter is, the better the response you will get. If it takes you ten pages to convey the benefits of your practice, then take ten pages. The important thing is not the length of your document but the quality of your copywriting.

The late John Lennon, former Beatle and song writing legend, once said that whenever they wanted anything, they could sit down and "write themselves a swimming pool." What he meant was that their song-writing skills were so good that they could write a song guaranteed to produce massive sales.

Great copywriting can have a similar effect on your veterinary business. A well crafted letter can produce a flood of new income to your practice. The perfect direct response letter will make the recipient want to jump out of that cozy armchair by the fire and rush out into the freezing snow in dressing gown and slippers to get the family pet to your practice.

Copywriting is a skill that must be learned, and there are entire books and courses on this subject alone. Don't approach this casually. Either hire a copywriter to write your letters for you, learn the basics yourself (see Resources), or delegate that responsibility to a member of your team who has learned at least the basics.

The good news is that copywriting is a skill that almost anyone can learn, so investing some time and money will usually ensure that it is skill you can have within your practice.

As a guide, here are our Top Ten copywriting tips for crafting a great letter:

1. Use a compelling headline.

2. Use subheads to create a double readership path. Some readers like to skim through letters, so sub-headings let you convey the gist of your letter to the recipient who won't read every word.

3. Make it about them not you; replace *we* and *our* with *you* and *your*.

4. Use client testimonials.

5. Use bullet points to highlight your benefits.

6. Make a compelling offer.

7. Give a guarantee. Guarantees are good way to reverse any risk your prospect perceives in connection with responding to your offer.

8. Use a deadline or scarcity warning.

9. Use graphics to highlight key parts of your letter.

10. Use a P.S. Some readers may skip straight to the end of your letter, so think of the post script as a second headline.

2. Postcards

Postcards can be effective because they do not have to be opened to be read and they are extremely cheap to produce. Do not make the mistake of imitating everyone else, who wastes space by covering most of the card with photos.

A good postcard must have a large compelling headline to grab recipients' attention and give them a reason to pick it up. Rather than using the standard postcard size (4.25" x 6"), you should use larger sized postcards that will stand out from other mail. The Post Office prices postage according to the size and thickness of the postcard. Usually a fixed amount of postage will cover postcards between a minimum and maximum size; we recommend using the maximum size allowed within the range.

It is now just as easy to have your printer personalize your copy with the recipients' names as it is to print their names and addresses, so by all means, personalize your copy. As prescribed by our direct response guidelines, you need to include a compelling offer and a deadline to encourage timely response.

Of course, with a postcard, you're never sure which side will be seen first, so for maximum response you should have the recipient's name, your offer, and the deadline on both sides of the card.

Postcards usually have not gotten as good a response as the long-copy sales letter. If you send them as part of a multi-step sequence, however, their return on investment justifies their cost of production, which is relatively low.

Furthermore, advanced printing processes allow you now to do some really cool things with postcards to connect with your prospects and increase your response rate. For example, you can enhance your personal message to each reader, perhaps by showing a photo of dog bowl with the recipient's dog's name on it.

You can also make postcards interactive by adding scratch-off panels similar to lottery scratch cards. This is a fun way to create an offer. As a general rule of thumb, the more senses you stimulate in your recipients and the more interaction they have with your postcards, the more engaged they will be with your message and the more likely they will be to respond.

An additional use for postcards is to drive prospects to your Website. You see, while direct mail is really powerful, even postcards have some associated expense. However, when you can get a prospect to your Website, where you can get an e-mail address and/or telephone number, you put yourself in a position to do your marketing in other less expensive ways.

The advancement of variable data printing technology has created some exciting new opportunities for marketers. The latest of these and most exciting is the ability to print Personalized URLs (PURLs) on postcards. A PURL is a Web address personalized to an individual, for example, johnsmith.xyzveterinarypractice.com or alternatively www.xyzveterinarypractice.com/johnsmith.

A PURL can be generated for each person on your mailing list and then printed on the postcard you send. The purpose of the postcard is to highlight the PURL with an offer awarded for visiting it. The curiosity factor alone is enough to prompt a visit to the special personalized Website.

The message on the Website can be tailored to the recipient and can be much longer than could have fitted on a postcard. This is a very powerful strategy to employ as a personal message, much more powerful than a "Dear Pet Owner" message. It is also an advanced strategy and one that will require some help and guidance from your printer.

3. Tear Sheets

A tear sheet is a mail piece disguised to look like a page that has been torn out of a newspaper or magazine. It usually takes the form of an article that appears to have been written about your practice and could include an ad that you have created actually to go into a real magazine or newspaper.

Tear sheets are very effective because properly done they appear to recipients as something sent by a friend who has read the article and is recommending that they read it too. They are also very rarely used, so you can be fairly sure that your prospects will not have seen this type of mailing.

For maximum covert effect, the tear sheet is usually sent out with a hand-written sticky note attached to the front that says something along the lines of:

It's signed off as "J" because—let's face it—everyone knows someone whose first name begins with the letter J!

The folded tear sheet, with sticky note attached, is then sent in a plain white hand-addressed envelope with one or more real postage stamps affixed. A plain #10 envelope with a hand-written address and real stamps is almost certain to be opened by the recipient.

The tear sheet copy itself should have the compelling headline, irresistible offer, and call to action, but it should appear to have been written by a third party. Your actual tear sheet will look not dissimilar to the direct response ad in Figure 3 in Chapter 9, except that it will be laid out in newspaper column style.

Done correctly, it will appear to be a newspaper article rather than an advertisement. You can further enhance this illusion by heading the first column with a columnist's name, for example:

By James Brown
SYNDICATED COLUMNIST

As with our advertorial newspaper ads, in order to comply with Federal Trade Commission regulations, you must put the word "advertisement" in the top margin above the headline. It has been proven repeatedly that this is unlikely to have any effect on your response rate, because most people will be attracted to your headline first and then start reading down.

Your local printer may not have heard of tear sheets, but there are printers who actually specialize in them (see Resources section) and can fulfill the whole process, including laying out your tear sheet copy to look like a newspaper article, applying hand written sticky notes, hand-addressing your envelopes, applying stamps, and mailing them for you.

Remember the hurdles direct mail has to clear? Letters, postcards, or tear sheets—they must be delivered, they must be opened, and they must be read. There is one more thing that each requires, and that is follow-up. **The worst number in direct mail is 1.**

The biggest mistake you can make with direct mail is sending just one piece. Most businesses that try direct mail send out one letter and then stop if they don't see immediate results. That's like exercising for one day and then stopping because you didn't lose all the weight you hoped you would!

In order to get results, you must do a direct mail campaign, which we define as being at least three sequential mailings, either of the same type or a combination of letters, postcards, and tear sheets. Furthermore, all your advertising and mail pieces should be traceable.

If you want your prospective client to call you, then use a different call-back number for each campaign (you can buy numbers that can be monitored) or give the recipient a call-in code to quote. This will help you track the response. If you're sending recipients to your Website, then send them to a page that has been set up specifically for that campaign.

Finally, if you are planning to mail out to a large number of people, test your mail pieces on a smaller list first, e.g., between 500 and 2,500, and track their responses. This will give you an indication of how successful a bigger campaign might be and save you money if your campaign isn't going to be the home run you hoped for.

To Find What Works Best, Measure and Test!

CHAPTER 11
INTERNET MARKETING

The Internet is becoming the town square for the global village of tomorrow.

–Bill Gates

Believe it or not, the Internet has become the number one source of information. Whereas twenty years ago most people would use the Yellow Pages to create a shortlist of possible veterinary practices, today they turn to Google® to research pet health issues and to find a veterinarian. This cannot be ignored by any veterinary practice owner who wishes to stay competitive. The simple fact is that for many people...**if you don't have a Website, you don't exist!**

Despite this, the shocking reality is that many veterinary practices do not have Websites, and for many that do, the Web brings them no business at all or they have no way to measure how much!

A quick Google® search for vets in your area (type "Veterinary Clinics near <YOUR City>") will show you a selection of Websites that vary widely in quality. Most of these Websites (even the good ones) appear to be modeled on a paper brochure. They itemize the services of the practice and give driving directions to the clinic, decorated with cute pictures of puppies. Some of these Websites look good, although most really don't, but the important question is this: do they attract new clients?

What is the purpose of your Website? It should address four objectives:

1. To give your clients and prospects something to enhance their client experience.

2. To sell goods or services.

3. To encourage clients and prospects to make appointments or make inquiries.

4. To collect the contact information you can use to add prospects to your marketing pool for products and services.

That's it!

If your Website does none of these four things, it does NOT generate business for you. (If there are exceptions to this rule, they are by good luck and not by good management.)

You may have heard that Websites serve a brand building purpose, and that can be true. That is a by-product, however, not a goal of the Website. Be under no illusions: your Website is there to attract new clients and keep existing ones. It should be as accountable for those results as any live salesperson would be.

If your Website is not pulling its weight, systematically helping to attract and keep clients, then you need to change it right now. Every day you delay is a day that is costing you money, a day that you are leaving thousands of dollars on the table.

In this chapter, we'll show you how you can make the Internet work for your practice by implementing an Internet-based Client Attraction System with your Website at its core.

The Website Client Attraction System

If yours is like many veterinary practices, your Website is just a digital version of your practice brochure. It sits in lonely isolation on the Internet and is looked at only by people whom you have asked to look at it! You may advertise your Web address on your business cards and the sides of your vehicles, but you'd be surprised how many vets don't even do this much self-promotion. Even if you do, however, this kind of advertising will generally account for very few visitors to your Website.

Most practices approach their Website design with the attitude that "if you build it, they will come." This fosters the natural inclination of Web design companies to concentrate on building attractive-looking Websites rather than building in a system to make them work. Aesthetics have the WOW Factor that tickles a client's fancy, and most Web companies have a design background rather than a process background, so it's up to you to assure that your Website serves its purpose.

Just having a Website is not enough. A digital version of your practice brochure will not attract new clients, but a direct response marketing Website will.

A system for attracting new clients via your Website will have the four main components shown in figure 6.

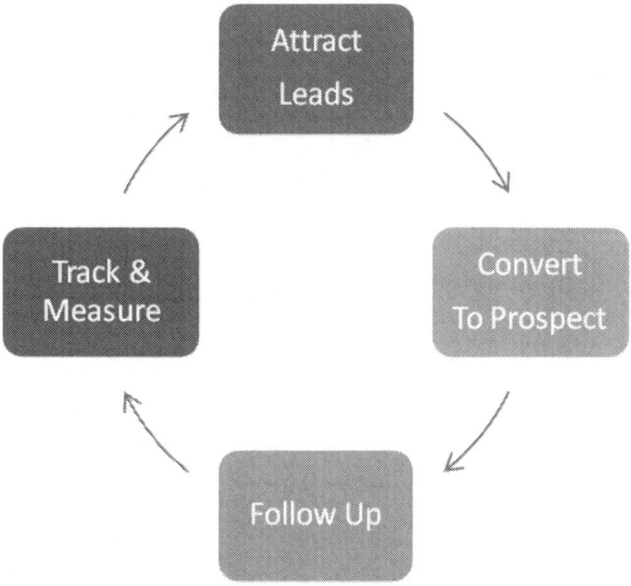

Figure 6 - The Website Client Attraction System

Think of these components like wheels on a car. Each is as important as the others. All necessary to keep your Website Client Attraction System moving.

Website System—Step 1
Attract Leads to Your Website

Without visitors (or traffic, in Internet jargon) your Website is useless. You might have the prettiest Website on the Net, loaded with special effects, but if nobody ever visits it, then what's the point? If the visitors to your Website are not interested in your product or service, that isn't much better.

What you really need are "leads," visitors who come to your Website because they believe that they will find a solution to their need or problem.

In order to attract leads to your Website, you can either buy traffic or grow traffic! Some Websites are good sources of leads, and you can pay to advertise with them, or you can develop strategies to locate your Website organically on search engines and other free Websites.

Buying Website Traffic

Buying traffic is by far the quickest way to start getting leads to your Website. You can literally put up an ad and have leads visiting your Website within hours.

There are three main sources of paid traffic:

1. **Search Engines** such as Google®

2. **Social Media Sites** such as Facebook®

3. **Banner Ads** placed directly on other Websites

Each of these sources works a little differently from the others, so let's look more closely at each one in turn. We'll take them in order of their popularity as sources of Internet advertising.

Buying Ads on Search Engines

For the sake of simplicity, let's examine the Google® search engine as our model for this source of Internet advertising. Google will allow you to create mini advertisements that appear for a given search term.

These are called Sponsored Links and appear either across the top or down the right-hand side of the search page. Google's sponsored links are commonly referred to as Google® AdWords.

The basic concept is that you bid an amount per click (hence the terms Pay Per Click or PPC) for your advert to appear on the first page of Google® for the searched Keyword or Phrase. Most people think that the more you pay, the higher on the list you will appear, and this does play a part. However, there are other factors that come into play, and it is quite common for a higher-paid ad to be listed lower than one that cost less.

This is because Google is concerned with "Keyword Relevance." They want the person doing the search to have the best possible user experience so they will continue to use Google. Keyword relevance is intended to increase the chances that ad appearing for a given keyword will be relevant to that keyword and that the Webpage those ads point to are also relevant.

To ensure this happens, Google evaluates your ad relative to the keyword or phrase you are bidding on. They will actually assign each a quality score from 1 to 10 and penalize you if your quality score is too low. The quality score is based on the relevance of your ad to the keyword, the relevance of your Website to the keyword, and the loading speed of your Website. (They don't want to invite their users to a site that requires waiting five minutes while your Website loads!)

Another factor affecting the quality score is the Click Thru Rate or CTR, the number of clicks on your ad as a percentage of the number of times it has appeared. E.g. If your advert had appeared 100 times and been clicked on twice, then your CTR would be 2%. To Google, a higher CTR indicates greater relevance, as determined by user interest (clicks).

Obviously, the more relevant the keywords you bid on are to the services or products you provide, the better the quality of leads you will attract. It is also worth pointing out that you can also specify words that you do <u>not</u> want your ads connected to.

For example, you can exclude appearance in response to keywords such as "Free" and "Cheap" as part of the keyword phrase. If a pet owner is searching for "cheap vet," you don't want to be in the search results!

Making AdWords Work for Your Veterinary Practice

There are four keys to making Google® AdWords work for your veterinary practice:

1. **Make Your Ad Specific to Your Keywords**

Since Google wants to ensure that your ad is specific to the keyword or keywords being searched, it is a big mistake to use the same ad for every keyword you bid on, like one-size-fits-all example:

XYZ Veterinary Clinic
We Get Your Pet Feeling Healthy.
$10 Off First Pet Exam.
www.XYZVeterinaryClinic.com

If the keyword phrase were veterinary clinic, then this ad would be fine. If the keyword phrase was "dog has bad breath," then the ad is not specific enough.

The person searching knows the dog could be seen by a vet but is doing some preliminary investigation into the problem's possible causes and solutions. Your job is to be the one to provide the information and solutions. The strategy here is to create a bond of trust with your prospects by filling their needs. This makes the job of converting a prospect to a paying client a whole lot easier.

In this instance, a more useful ad for the phrase

"dog has bad breath" might look like this:

> Your Dog Has Bad Breath?
> It May Mean Your Dog Is Unwell!
> *Free Report Reveals Warning Signs*
> www.XYZVeterinaryClinic.com

You can see that the ad couldn't be more relevant to the search phrase. It even has the actual search phrase in the title.

Another bonus is that whenever your ad uses any of the keywords being searched, they will be highlighted in **bold** print when they appear in the search results. In this example, the words **Dog Has Bad Breath** in the headline of your ad would appear bold to make your ad stand out from the others.

2. Make Your Landing Page Specific to Your Keywords

To complete the user experience, Google wants your ad to send the searcher to a landing page (your Webpage) that is relevant to the keywords originally searched. This is to prevent the bait-and-switch tactics employed by unscrupulous advertisers who lure the searcher with one thing and then offer something entirely different on the landing page.

While we do not expect veterinary practices to use these kinds of tactics, a common mistake they do make is to send the searcher to their veterinary Website home page no matter what keywords were searched.

In the bad dog breath scenario, for example, a more relevant place to send the searcher would be to a page on your Website that was specifically about the causes of bad breath in dogs and some related symptoms. Because this page is more relevant than your home page (which is unlikely to mention anything about bad breath in dogs), Google will very likely award a higher quality score for these keywords. This means your ads will be less expensive and could actually cost less than other ads placed lower for the same keywords.

3. Test Multiple Ads for Each Keyword Theme

One of the clever things that Google® AdWords lets you do is to test multiple adverts for the same keywords. For example, in our dog-breath scenario we could test the following two ads for the keywords "dog has bad breath":

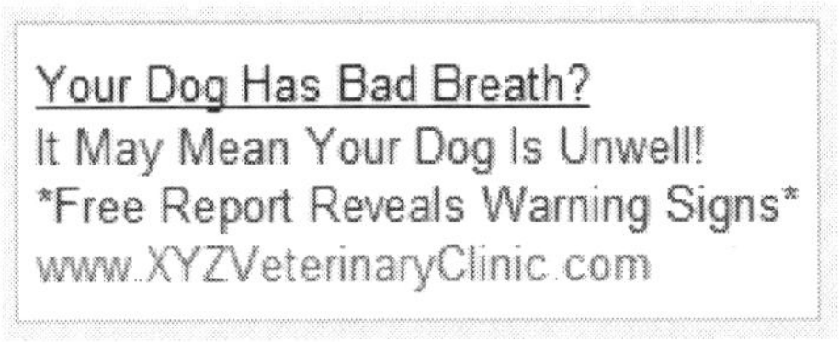
Your Dog Has Bad Breath?
It May Mean Your Dog Is Unwell!
Free Report Reveals Warning Signs
www.XYZVeterinaryClinic.com

Sick Of Dog's Bad Breath?
It May Mean Your Dog Is Unwell!
Free Report Reveals Warning Signs
www.XYZVeterinaryClinic.com

The only difference between the ads is the headline. This is not an accident: you should test only one part of your ad at a time so that you know specifically which change has made the difference. Google will automatically take turns running the two ads and tell you which one has had the best CTR. Once you have established whether there is a clear winner, you can replace the losing ad with another one and start another test.

This may seem like a lot of work, but it's worth it. The better click-through-rate you can achieve, the cheaper your clicks will become.

4. **Track Your Results**

The final key to making Google® AdWords work for your practice is to make sure you track the results. Google will tell you how many times each of your ads has been clicked on for each of the keyword phrases you are bidding on. You want to track which of these clicks resulted in a new prospect raising a hand, a new client joining the practice, or the searcher buying something from your Website.

Google will help by giving you tracking codes for each Webpage you want to track. This means that for each keyword, you can see whether the person who clicked on your ad signed up for your free report example or bought some dental chews from you online.

It is harder to track whether a searcher joins your practice as a result of clicking on your ad. It can be done though, as you will see in the section on tracking and measuring at the end of this chapter.

Tip: You should also adjust your bids frequently to ensure that you are not paying too much for ad that have good placements and not paying too little for ads that are not but could be appearing on page one of Google®. This is because the number of clicks you receive (your click-thru-rate) and the ongoing arrival of new bidders makes the ad positions a moving target.

The Google® Content Network

Another way to use AdWords is the Google® Content Network. Google allows Website owners to run Google® AdWords advertisements on their Websites and pays a commission when someone clicks on these ads.

The good thing about this is that if you are running an ad on the Content Network, you can choose which Websites you want your ads to appear on. So you identify which Websites your potential clients are looking at, such as pages ranking high for relevant keywords, and put your ads there!

A warning here though is that if you do not target Websites with a local focus, you could end up wasting a lot of money on people who click your advert from the other side of the country.

Facebook Ads

Facebook® is now the most used Website in the world and a very powerful tool for finding clients. Look at these figures:

- At time of writing, Facebook had more than 133,690,220 active users in the USA. That's a staggering 44% of the US Population! In other words, nearly half your clients and half your prospective clients are likely to be using Facebook!

- Fifty per cent of active users log on to Facebook in any given day! So nearly a quarter of your clients and prospects are on Facebook every single day!

- The average Facebook user has 130 Friends! That means for every 1,000 clients you have, there may be 130,000 prospects hearing good (or not so good) things about your practice!

In June 2010, The Nielsen Company reported that Facebook users spent an average of 6 hours 2 minutes 59 seconds on Facebook per month; that's over 12 minutes per day. While that might not sound like a lot, it is more than Google, eBay, and Amazon combined!

The biggest difference between advertising on Facebook and advertising on Google® is this: with Google® your leads find you, with Facebook you find your leads.

For example, if you wanted to target people with an interest in dogs within a 25-mile radius of your practice, Facebook will easily let you do this.

Facebook ads also differ from Google® Ads because they allow you to use an image and more text. Here is an example of how a Facebook ad might look for our dog-breath scenario:

As you can see, Facebook ads look very different from Google® Ads. Here are our top 3 tricks for creating a Facebook Ad:

1. Use an eye-catching image to grab the attention of the Facebook users you are targeting. Your ad will be competing with other ads for their attention, so make it stand out.

2. Ask a question in your title to qualify them. Advertising on Facebook is a bit like advertising in a newspaper or magazine, so you want to make sure your audience is left in no doubt who the ad is aimed at. You also don't want people clicking the ad if they don't fit your criteria; every click costs money!

3. Make a promise or offer so there's good a reason to click on your ad. The example above offers a free report as an incentive.

It is a good idea to ensure that the image you use in the ad also appears somewhere on the landing page. This reassures users that they will be getting what they clicked for and not be subjected to bait and switch tactics.

We advise you initially to send the searcher to your Facebook fan page rather than to your Website, because Facebook users will feel more comfortable within the Facebook environment. We will discuss the content of your Facebook page and of your Website in the "Convert to Prospect" section of this chapter.

Banner Ads

A banner ad is a pictorial advertisement that you place on someone else's Website. You may have seen them on one of the veterinary trade magazine Websites for pharmaceutical products or a brand of pet food. While the ads on these sites are obviously aimed at veterinarians, Figure 7 shows a typical pet-related banner ad aimed at pet owners.

Figure 7 - Horizontal Banner Ad

Although the horizontal banner ad is without doubt the most common banner ad you will see, it is not the only type available to you as an advertiser. Vertical banner ads are also common, and so are various sizes of rectangular and square banner ads.

Figure 8 shows a typical pet-related square banner ad.

Figure 8 - Square Banner Ad

Banner ads work in a similar way to Google's Content Network ads in that they are effectively advertisements on other people's Websites.

With banner ads, however, you have more control over how they're distributed.

- You can pay Website owners directly to display your banner on their sites. This usually works well on local business Websites.

- You can join a banner exchange that allows you to advertise other companies' Websites in return for them advertising yours. We do not recommend this option, as it encourages your visitors to click on something that will take them elsewhere.

- You can use a Banner Network (similar to the Google® Content Network) to have your ad automatically displayed on other Websites.

You usually pay for banner ads per 1000 impressions (per 1000 times your ad is seen on other Websites) or per month if you are paying the Website owner directly. Banner ads can be static images or animated (i.e. several different images appearing sequentially within the same image space).

By targeting Websites specific to your service or product, you can attract quality leads. For example, your local pet rescue center or pet boutique is likely to have the same clients and prospective clients as your veterinary practice. Therefore, it is worth approaching them and enquiring how many visitors they get to their Websites each month.

You could then negotiate with them to place a banner ad for your practice on one of their Websites, or both, at a price appropriate to the number of visitors expected to see it.

Tip: While advertising on other Websites can be a great source of leads for your own Website, you should not put others' ads on your Website. Except for a third-party pet portal service for your clients, you never want your visitors to click on anything that will take them away from your Website.

The takeaway to buying traffic is that it will attract leads to your Website quickly, in some cases within minutes, but at a cost.

Growing Website Traffic

Growing your own Website traffic is by far the cheapest method of getting traffic to your Website, but it can take some time to produce results. By growing traffic, we mean finding visitors from places on the Internet that are free!

There are five main sources of FREE traffic:

1. Organic Search Engine Listings
2. Google® Places (Maps) Listing
3. Article Submissions
4. Video Submissions
5. Social Media

1. Organic Search Engine Listings

When you type a phrase into a search engine, two types of results come back, the sponsored ads we already discussed and links to Websites that the search engine determines to be relevant.

These latter offerings are often called "organic" results because they cannot be bought but can only be attained by nurturing a Website to ensuring that it has everything the search engines require to place it on the first page.

Your Website will exhibit three characteristics if it is to do well organically:

1. It will be well structured and optimized for your desired keywords.

2. It will frequently display new content.

3. It will have incoming links (or back links) from other Websites.

Let's look at each one of these features in turn.

Well structured and optimized for your desired keywords

There are several places your keywords should appear within your Website.

Your site will consist of a primary keyword such as "[City Name] Vet" and some secondary keywords such as "[City Name] Dog Grooming," "[City Name] Boarding Kennels," "Itchy Dog," etc. Each secondary keyword should have its own Webpage.

Your Domain Name, if possible, should include your primary keyword; e.g., start with your town/city name and then the word vet or animal hospital.

There are also several places within the code that makes up your website that your keyword(s) relating to each page should appear such as your page title. Any decent Website designer should have this in hand.

You should have links at the foot of your page to a Privacy Policy page, which explains that you will not abuse any e-mail addresses or other personal details collected on your site. A Terms & Conditions page is also a good idea.

Frequent new content

Search engines favor sites that are updated frequently. They assume that sites that have remained static are out of date and, therefore, no longer relevant. You should be updating your site monthly as a matter of course, with new offers, product information or advisories, staff birthdays, articles, client testimonials, and referral thank you messages.

An easy way to ensure weekly or even daily fresh content is to have a blog on your site. If your Website uses the WordPress platform, then you can add a blog in a matter of seconds. Your blog should contain useful information for your clients and interesting news about your practice and the personalities within it, i.e., you and your staff.

Each blog post need only be around 100 to 200 words (It sounds a lot but it isn't; there are more words than that on this page.) and wherever possible should contain some of your keywords with a link to the relevant page.

Learning to do this is not an overnight process and can involve a lot of specialized work, but the rewards can be enormous if you get your Website onto the first or second page of Google® without having to pay for the privilege! It effectively gives you a huge advantage over your competitors. If they have to pay for their ads, then they are incurring a cost that you don't have; if they aren't there at all, then they won't be found!

Incoming links (or back links) from other Websites

When we talk about back links, we are really talking about links from Websites that the search engines classes as "authority" sites or from the Websites of other local area businesses.

Believe it or not, Google actually ranks every Webpage (that's Webpage not Website) that they have indexed on a scale from 0 (unranked) to 10. The higher the rank, the higher the "authority" Google assigns the page. The higher the rank, the greater the value of the link to your Website. Also the more links your Webpage receives, the greater the rank Google will assign to your Webpage.

Only Google knows for sure how they assign weights, but there are many theories about it. For example, it is widely thought that to get a page rank (PR) of 3, your page would need either 555 links from pages on other sites with PR1 or just one link from a page with PR5!

This means that links from other high-ranking sites mean higher rankings for you in the search engines. There are free tools available to reveal the page rank of any Webpage including yours.

There are also some other sites that whose links Google® values above others:

- Government Websites (.gov)
- School & University Websites (.edu)
- Local Business Websites (your local chiropractor, beauty spa, dentist, realtor, etc.)

2. Google® Places

Google® Places a free service Google provides for local businesses. Whenever you search in Google® for a local business (e.g. Veterinary Practices) in your area, you are likely to see a small map appear, accompanied by a list of businesses. For example, Lake Mary, FL Veterinary brings the following results:

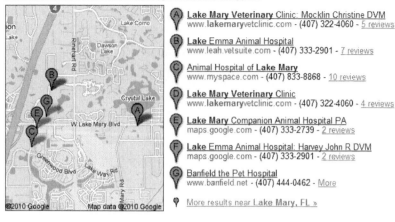

Local business results for **veterinary** near **Lake Mary, FL**

A **Lake Mary Veterinary** Clinic: Mocklin Christine DVM
www.**lakemaryvetclinic**.com - (407) 322-4060 - 5 reviews

B **Lake** Emma Animal Hospital
www.leah.vetsuite.com - (407) 333-2901 - 7 reviews

C Animal Hospital of **Lake Mary**
www.myspace.com - (407) 833-8868 - 10 reviews

D **Lake Mary Veterinary** Clinic
www.**lakemaryvetclinic**.com - (407) 322-4060 - 4 reviews

E **Lake Mary** Companion Animal Hospital PA
maps.google.com - (407) 333-2739 - 2 reviews

F **Lake** Emma Animal Hospital: Harvey John R DVM
maps.google.com - (407) 333-2901 - 2 reviews

G Banfield the Pet Hospital
www.banfield.net - (407) 444-0462 - More

More results near **Lake Mary, FL** »

If your listing has not been claimed, then it will show maps.google.com as the Website. The position of your listing is based on the following:

1. How complete your actual listing is.

2. The keywords included in your company information.

3. Your actual Website optimization, with city and state keywords in title, description, and your actual address listed on the site.

4. Category with the search terms listed.

5. Proximity to center of your city.

6. Extra style: photos, videos, directions, etc. (things that dress up your listing).

7. Listings in other directories that include local address info such as Yelp, City Search, Verizon, Yahoo, Local Online Yellow Pages, All Pages, Local.com, etc.

8. Number of inbound back links from other local directories.

9. Actual total number of reviews.

10. High/Solid ratings in your Google® reviews—the more stars, the better your listing.

It is also possible to add vouchers to your listing that prospective clients can use in your practice and that will also increase your visibility.

3. Article Submissions

Many Websites publish informational articles on the Internet. Some, such as EzineArticles.com, publish articles on a wide variety of topics; others are specific to a particular niche or industry. It is usually free to post articles on these sites, and in most cases, the footer of your article can include a link back to your own Website. This is great for two reasons.

First, you can post an article about the solution that your service or product provides, that then allows the reader to click a link taking them directly to your Website. Someone who has searched the article site looking for a solution to a problem, then looked at your article, and then clicked the link to visit your Website, is almost certainly an interested visitor rather than someone who has stumbled onto your Website by mistake.

Second, these links back to your Website are exactly what search engines are looking for, so they will help your search engine ranking.

If you have written papers or newspaper articles on a particular topic, such as pet dentistry, then these can be used for article submissions.

4. Video Submissions

As technology has advanced and sites such as YouTube (now a Google company) have emerged, Video has become a significant part of the Internet world. There are lots of Websites where you can submit videos about your product or service to help drive traffic to your Website and spread your message TV-style.

Google® loves video, and when you do it correctly, you can dominate the first page of Google® with video for the relevant keywords, especially for local searches. To get your videos on Google® quickly, use YouTube.

Of course, your YouTube.com videos can also be embedded in your Website. For example, video testimonials from your clients are a great addition to your Website.

YouTube will actually let you set up your own channel, such as www.youtube.com/xyzveterinary, to keep all your videos in one place for public consumption.

5. Social Media

Social media, as the term suggests, are Websites such as Facebook, MySpace, and Twitter, where users socialize. The key to marketing at social media sites is not to push your products and services from these sites directly but to build rapport and gain recognition as an expert. Once you have gained the trust, then you can invite them to your Website where you offer your services.

Think of social media as a way for people to interact with each other online and, more importantly for you, as a way for veterinary practices to interact with their prospects and clients online.

Types of Social Media Website

There are thousands of social media Websites, but there are only three types of social media that veterinarians need to embrace.

Social Networking Sites

Examples: Facebook.com, Twitter.com

Social networking sites are where groups of individuals come together online to socialize with one another. Social networks such as Facebook can be used by people who share the same interests or for socializing online with friends and family. Others are for following the updates of people you have an interest in, as is the case with Twitter.

Social Bookmarking Sites

Examples: Delicious.com, Digg.com, and Stumbleupon.com

Social bookmarking sites allow users to bookmark Websites for easy reference later, similar to clicking favorite to mark a Website on your personal computer. The big difference is that the favorites saved on your personal computer are private, but these social bookmarks are shared with others across the Internet. So even if your Website is not ranking particularly high in the search engines, if you bookmark your site it could be seen by others who use the social bookmarking sites.

Social Media Sharing Sites

Examples:
Blogs—WordPress, Blogger
Photo Sharing—Flickr
Video Sharing—YouTube, Google® Video etc
Presentation Sharing—Scribd

Social media sharing sites are now extremely popular because they allow people to share information in writing and also in the form of photos, videos, and audio recordings. Users can interact and express their views on these sites through comments and votes.

Blogs

The term "blog" is short for Web log and is really just an online journal where a user's thoughts are published to the world. You can set up blogs sites such as WordPress.com and Blogger.com, but it benefits your business most if your blog is part of your Website.

WordPress can be installed on your Website at no cost, and it is extremely easy to use, so be sure to ask your Website designer to install it for you.

An important reason to have your blog on your Website is that search engines love sites that are constantly being updated regularly (it shows they are fresh and not out-of-date) and sites that are growing. One of the easiest ways to achieve both is to maintain a blog that by its very nature serves both purposes.

Photo Sharing, Video Sharing, & Presentation Sharing

Do not underestimate the power of video media sharing sites. YouTube plays over two **billion** videos every day worldwide, and 30% of YouTube traffic is from the US!

The most compelling fact about YouTube, however, is that it is the #2 search engine behind Google®! So it goes without saying that thousands of pet owners will be searching YouTube every day in search of solutions to everyday pet problems, such as how to check a dog's teeth (346 videos uploaded at time of writing) or how to express a dog's anal glands (57 videos uploaded).

Facebook

Although Facebook does not allow businesses as members, it is possible to create a page for your business under your personal membership.

After you have done this, the next step is to get as many people as possible to 'like' your page by clicking the 'like' button on your fan page. Once you have 25 fans or more, you can apply to have your own free Facebook URL (e.g., www.facebook.com/yourveterinarypractice).

Update your Facebook page with information likely to be of interest to your fans. In other words, don't just try to sell them stuff!

Facebook pages have a tabbed interface that can be used to focus attention on important elements of your page. You can create tabs for things like videos, photos, discussion, and events, and by doing so you can build out subpages with a specific focus. These tabs use common Facebook applications, such as Events, to drive the page content and are simple to set up and edit.

Each tab has a unique URL, giving you the ability to promote particular events or photos as well as to create some custom landing-page functionality. Note: the URLs for each tab can be long and cumbersome, so it may be worth buying a shorter and more relevant domain name that redirects to your Facebook page.

Facebook also has its own form of HTML code (computer code used to build Websites) called FBML which allows you (or your Web designer) to enhance the appearance of your Facebook tabs by adding buttons, opt-in forms, videos, and almost anything else that you can put on a Website.

Twitter

Twitter is a Website that allows you to broadcast messages to your "followers" in real time. The main benefit of this is that you can get information out quickly.

You should join Twitter and get your own Twitter page (e.g. www.twitter.com/yourveterinarypractice) as this will allow you to "tweet" to current and potential clients. A tweet is the Twitter message, limited to 140 characters, which is usually about a sentence.

Although, Twitter can seem like a pointless activity, there are actually a couple of real benefits:

1. If your tweet contains a link back to your Website, it will be regarded with high value by Google®, as Twitter has a very high page rank.

2. By putting the pound symbol in front of a word (e.g., #veterinarian), you can tag it so that it can be used to find you. The Twitter community use tagged words as search terms.

One of the easiest ways that we have found to update Twitter is to subscribe to a site such as twitterfeed.com, which will and automatically tweet your blog posts.

Getting It All Done

Keeping social media sites up to date can be time consuming, but there are now services to help you. For example, Posterous.com allows you to update Facebook, Twitter, Delicious, YouTube, Flickr, and many other social media sites, including your own blog, by sending just one e-mail! This means it's possible to update all your social media Websites in just 15 to 30 minutes a day.

Growing Traffic will attract leads to your Website more slowly than buying it, but it requires no cash outlay and takes little more time and attention.

Website System—Step 2
Convert Visitor to Prospect

Did you know that when someone visits your Website you have less than 5 seconds to grab their attention before they are ready to try something else? It is therefore important that the first page they see at your Website is not only relevant to what they're seeking but also interests them sufficiently to keep them there.

You need to define clearly what you want the visitor to do upon arriving at your Website. Remember, you have four objectives:

1. Give a current client or new lead something to enhance their experience with your practice.

2. Sell a product or service.

3. Make an appointment or answer an enquiry.

4. Get detailed information that will support future marketing efforts.

Let's examine Objective #4 now. This objective is most concerned with turning an interested visitor—a lead—into someone likely to buy in the future— a prospect.

To achieve this, four elements should be included on the pages where visitors first arrive at your Website, your landing pages. The four indispensable elements we recommend are:

1. A good headline.

2. A video introduction.

3. Relevant content optimized to the keywords that were most likely to have led to the page.

4. A form to capture the visitor's name and e-mail address so that you can send the information they request. Ideally, you will also obtain a mailing address so you can send your letters and postcards.

1. A Good Headline

If you have less than five seconds to grab your visitor's attention, a relevant and well-crafted headline is essential to keep interest and encourage further investigation.

For example, if your practice were based in Orlando and the visitor had found your site by typing "Orlando Veterinary Practice" into Google®, then your landing page might want a headline like this:

For Pet Owners: Who Else Puts Their Pets in the Care of Orlando's Leading Veterinary Practice?

OR

Warning For Orlando Pet Owners: Reading This Webpage Could Save Your Pet's Life!

Either of these headlines will grab the visitor's attention and keep him or her on your page.

2. A Video Introduction

It is now so easy to record video and put it on your Website that not having a video introduction classifies your site automatically as second-rate. As the popularity YouTube shows, people respond to video, so good-quality video on your landing page will induce your Website visitors to stay and also to interact with your Website.

This gives you the perfect opportunity to show prospective clients what a professional and caring veterinarian you are, while you convey the unique benefits of joining your practice.

3. Compelling and Relevant Content

If your visitor is to take the action you hope for, your page content obviously has to be compelling. Less obvious is that your landing page has to be keyword relevant. If you are driving traffic to your Website from Google® Adwords or from organic search engine listings, then it is extremely important these programs find your page.

In the previous example above, the landing-page text should be specific to the phrase "Orlando veterinary practice." That means the phrase "veterinary practice" must appear on your page a certain number of times.

You can't just throw it in there, though. Google® also uses a technique called Latent Semantic Indexing (LSI) to attempt to verify that sites have been written by humans and not by robots! LSI looks for other words that should be found where there are keywords. Therefore, in our example of the Orlando veterinary practice Webpage, LSI might also look for the following keywords:

- Veterinarian
- Animal
- Health
- Dog

- Cat
- Vaccination

As a rule of thumb, around 4 to 6% of the content needs to consist of the relevant and related keywords.

The more relevant the content is to the keywords that prospective clients are using to find you, the more likely they are to find you. Moreover, increasing relevant content increases your chance of appearing high in the search engines' lists and lowering your cost-per-click for paid traffic.

4. A Name/E-mail Address Capture Form

Now that your paid advertisements, organic search listings and/or article submissions have brought your visitor to a page on your Website,… Now that your headline has confirmed that this page might be of use to them and your content has kept their attention,… Now what?

Well, if you are v-e-r-y lucky, your visitor might pick up the phone and call you, send you an e-mail, or even visit your office. Human nature being what it is, it is far more likely that your visitor will either bookmark your site for "later," make a "mental note" to look you up again when there's more time or greater need, or write down your details and "file" (and forget) them.

Even if they like what they see, even if they have earmarked you as someone they would want to do business with, you will never know it. Even if you have Google® Analytics (see section on tracking) on your site, you will only know you've had visitors; frustratingly, you will not know who they were!) If pet owners are interested in your practice, you may never know who they were or what they wanted or how to get in touch with them.

The Name/E-mail Address Capture Form (sometimes referred to as the "Name Squeeze Page") can save you from this nightmare. The Name Squeeze Page (see figure 9) looks like just a couple of boxes on your Webpage that invite visitors to type in their Names and e-mail addresses. Underneath that is a button to press that sends the information to you. Your challenge is persuading your visitors to accept the invitation of these boxes.

Getting Visitors to Enter Their Details

Figure 9 - Website Capture Form

Why would a visitor to your Website use the data capture boxes? Well, the simple answer is that you make it worth their while; you offer something of value in return. Some visitors will be reluctant to give you their information. However, they may overcome their hesitation if you offer them a free report on something to do with your product or service, e.g., "The 5 Questions You Must Ask before Allowing a Vet to Examine Your Pet" or "How to Ensure Your Vet Will Make Your Pet Top Priority." Your job is to supply a reason for your visitor to share the information you want.

It doesn't have to be a report either; it just has to be

something of perceived value to the visitor. Competitions work well: "Enter your name and address for a chance to win a year's worth of free dog food etc"

What you are effectively asking them to do is raise a hand and say, "Yes, I'm interested in what you have to offer. Please send me more information." If the offer is targeted correctly to what they are looking for, then you will find that as many as 20-50% of your Website visitors will sign up.

It doesn't take a math genius to figure out that if you had 500 visitors to your Website every month, you could be adding 100 to 250 persons to your prospect list every month.

Tip: We have seen a few veterinary practices who offer a subscription to their eNewsletter as the giveaway. This usually isn't very effective. It is not sufficiently compelling, and pet owners are reluctant to commit to a monthly communication when they have no relationship with you.

A single free report that helps them solve a specific problem is an entirely different matter.

Ensuring the E-mail Address Is Genuine

One question you may be asking yourself is, "What if they just type in MickeyMouse@FantasyLand.com or some equally bogus e-mail address." Well, first of all, the report (or other inducement) is to be delivered (or announced) by e-mail, so only a valid e-mail address can receive it. Second, before the report is delivered, you will send an e-mail to confirm that the visitor wants to receive it.

The visitor only becomes a prospect, then, if the e-mail address is real and if and "opt-in" reply means your follow up e-mails aren't going to be treated as SPAM. (Your follow up e-mails will include a link that allows for removal from your distribution for any recipient who wants to opt out.)

Isn't This All a Bit Too Complicated?

By now you may be thinking that all this is much more easily said than done. Not so. (Ask our editor. It wasn't at all easy to say!) If you need assistance to implement these first two steps of our Website System, there are services available on the Internet that will do a lot of the work for you. We recommend that you check out Aweber.com, MailChimp.com, and Constant Contact.

These companies provide what is known in the Internet marketing industry as an auto-responder. It is an easy-to-use software program that creates the form you need for your Website and allows you to put the building of your prospect list and delivery of your e-mails on autopilot.

There's a saying in the Internet marketing world: "The money's in the list." We would modify that to say it's in the relationship you build with the list. Having a list of interested prospects that you can e-mail offers to is like gold dust in a mountain stream. With a big enough list and a suitable well-crafted offer, you can pan for real gold in that stream and bring surges of cash into your practice.

Website System—Step 3
Follow Up with Prospects

Once your newly acquired prospect has received the free report or other inducement, then you need to work on turning the prospect into a client, not forgetting that when that succeeds, you will need to work to make sure you keep that client.

It is generally accepted that it takes 7-9 contacts on average before a prospective client becomes a paying client. Sending one e-mail or report just isn't going to cut the mustard! Your objective should be to make sure that whenever your prospect is ready to become a client—today, next week, next month or even next year—yours is the practice that comes to mind. This applies whether or not there has already been a purchase.

How to Keep in Touch

In order to follow up properly, you need to send regular mailings, ideally once or twice a week. These mailings can include useful information, newsletters, news related to your practice, press releases, and (occasionally) offers.

Obviously, you do not want to spend all your time sending e-mails and, fortunately, you don't have to. The auto-responder software we mentioned above will let you preload a sequence of e-mails that it will deliver them automatically at times you specify. Just imagine being on vacation while your e-mails are delivered on your behalf and prospects are calling your practice to book appointments!

The auto-responder also allows you to send broadcast messages whenever you want to. If you want to send your list some urgent news, you don't have to schedule it around your other e-mails. You are free to use the means you choose to build a relationship with your prospect list and nurture your relationships with clients.

Naturally, as your prospect list grows you will be able to generate more new clients. Remember, you will be keeping in touch with hundreds of prospects who found your Website while looking for a service or product they needed, who then asked you to send them stuff! These are all potential clients.

The auto-responder gives you the leverage to interact with hundreds or thousands of prospective clients 24 hours a day, 7 days a week, without even having to be there!

Turning Prospects into Clients with Compelling Offers

Having hundreds of prospective clients on your e-mail list is great, but only as you can turn them into clients for your practice. You do this by interjecting into your informational e-mails compelling offers for your prospects.

If you keep your prospects and clients in separate e-mail lists, you can devise specific "new client only" offers that you e-mail to tempt prospects into your practice. As a rule of thumb, we suggest sending one offer every month to your prospects and sending informational, educational, or fun e-mails to them every week.

Remember, your prospects may not be ready to become clients this week, this month, or even this year, but by consistently providing them with great content and by making them great offers, you will find that when they are ready to change practices or join a practice for the first time, yours will be the one they think of first.

Website System—Step 4
Track & Measure

Most veterinary practices have no idea whether their Website is bringing in business. In fact, most businesses are unable to tell you with any degree of certainty whether any of their advertising is growing their business. Yes, they can tell you that business seemed to go up when they ran an ad in a couple of magazines, but they cannot say exactly how much business was generated or whether the ad was responsible for the increase.

To know whether your Client Attraction System is working, you need to measure and track your visitors, prospects, and sales.

You want to know that if you attract "V" number of visitors to your Website, you will get "M" number of them joining your mailing list and "C" number calling you, which will result in "S" number of sales. When you know these metrics and you know what the value of a client is to your business, then you can make informed decisions about how much you can afford to spend on paid traffic.

As important as knowing how much you can afford is knowing where you should spend your advertising budget. For example, with Google® Adwords it is important to spend your money on the keywords that are converting clicks into prospects and sales rather than the keywords that aren't getting you anywhere.

The key to this decision-making is to track everything and measure what the results of everything you try. You can then do more of the things that are working and less of the things that aren't!

Fortunately, Google® not only provides ways for you to track your Adwords but also has a free service called Google® Analytics that allows you to track the origin of your Website traffic. There are also simple things you can do yourself to track results.

For example, did you know that you can get a toll-free number that will automatically re-direct to your main phone line? By giving out a different number for each of your marketing activities, i.e., Website, Yellow Pages, newspaper ads, etc., you can track what is prompting your calls.

Tracking is vital to knowing whether your client-attracting efforts are working, either online or offline!

CHAPTER 12
REFERRAL PROGRAMS

*Loyal customers, they don't just come back,
they don't simply recommend you, they insist that their friends
do business with you.*

–Chip Bell

It is generally accepted that the best kind of new clients are those that have been referred by existing happy clients. They are far more receptive, more easily satisfied, and less price conscious.

That being the case, you want to know how well your referral system is working, which means how many of your new clients come from current client referrals. If you don't already know the answer, then make it a priority to start keeping track of who is referring, how many they refer, and how frequently they refer.

You also need to keep track of referral activity among staff. Which staff members are doing the most to encourage referrals, what are they doing, and how effective is it?

According to Joe Girard, the author of *How To Sell To Anybody*, the average number of attendees at both weddings and funerals is fifty-two. On that evidence he contends that each consumer has the potential to refer fifty-two other consumers.

You could argue that in the case of a veterinary practice this number would be less, as not all of the fifty-two will be pet owners. According to the U.S. Pet Ownership & Demographics Sourcebook (2007 Edition), 37.2% of U.S. households own dogs and 32.4% own cats. More recent statistics suggest that as many as 63% of U.S. households include a pet of some description. Of the 52 persons at the average funeral, then, one-third to two-thirds will be pet owners.

Erring on the side of caution, assuming only 25% pet ownership among your client's 52 friends and family, let us ask you this:

Is your practice averaging thirteen referrals per client?

The answer is probably not; in fact, most practices will average less than one referral per client, and some might not even get thirteen referrals altogether! Putting measures in place to generate referrals from your clients should be a key weapon in any veterinary practice's marketing arsenal. Getting your clients to make referrals is an underutilized but powerful strategy that can increase your practice size significantly.

Fact: the more referrals you get, the less you have to spend on marketing and advertising.

Just think, if you could get each of your clients to refer an average of just one pet-owning friend or family member to your practice, you would double the size of your practice! Your aim should be to create a clientele that is 50-80% referral-generated, meaning 50-80% of your new clients come by referral.

To make referrals an everyday event in your practice, there are four essential things you must do. We call them our Four Golden Keys to Client Referral. If you follow them, your referral numbers should be extremely healthy.

Four Golden Keys to Client Referral

How can you take your practice from averaging less than one referral per client to double-digit referrals per client? This chapter is devoted answering that question, showing you the four golden keys that will unlock the referral floodgates and condition your clients to be serial referrers.

Golden Referral Key #1

Give Them Something to Shout About!

First of all let us start by defining what we mean by *refer*. What we really mean is promote, and clients will not actively and abundantly promote your business unless you give them something worth promoting. That something is an experience so awe-inspiring and different from what they expect that they just can't help but tell everyone who will listen.

Clients do not enthusiastically refer the ordinary, the satisfactory, or even the above average. On the other hand, they irresistibly refer the outstanding, the unexpectedly wonderful, and the downright memorable.

You need to create a WOW Factor for your clients that will make your practice the talk of the town. If you can create the buzz, then your clients will be happy to convey their experience when they are meeting with friends, chatting with other parents at their kids' school soccer game, or talking to colleagues at work.

The late great Walt Disney once said:

Do what you do so well that they will want to see it again and bring their friends.

While we don't propose that you have Mickey Mouse inviting clients through your door (although it would be a memorable experience), we do recommend rethinking your customer experience, from the moment they pull up to park outside your practice to the moment they say good-bye.

What can you do in your practice today to enhance your clients' experience and give them something to shout about?

Don't think that providing a fantastic customer experience has to be expensive either. You can do a lot for little or no cost.Start with small things that are easy to implement yet make a big impact.

For example, could you give free dog and cat treats (palatable to all diets) for your patients?

Does your reception staff smile and look like they mean it when they speak to clients? A friendly face and tone of voice will put your clients at ease and make them feel welcome.

Does your staff always say please and thank you? This would be too obvious to mention if it were commonplace, but is rare enough to make a big contribution to creating a culture of referring.

What can you do to change the ambience of your waiting rooms and treatment rooms? Do they have to limit your practice to the usual basic, run-of-the-mill experience?

Can you get some murals painted on the walls, paint some clouds on the ceilings, or hang some amusing photos? What about displaying photos of the animals you care for?

Does your waiting room smell of disinfectant (or worse!) or does it have a more welcoming aroma?

Does your staff wear clinical, white uniforms or do you dress them in something equally professional but more attractive so that they look more approachable?

Are the magazines in your waiting room the latest issues of publications your clients might actually want to read? Are there enough to go around?

Do you offer your clients beverages and snacks while they are waiting for a veterinarian to see their pets?

When client buy large bags of dog food or other cumbersome products, do you have someone help carry it to the car?

When it's raining outside, is there an escort to the parking lot with an umbrella?

Have you surveyed your patients to ask what they think would improve their experience in your clinic?

A lot of apparently small changes can combine to create a big difference in your client's experience. How can you make your practice uniquely promotable?

Golden Referral Key #2

Ask Them!

As it says in a very old but very wise book, "Ask, and it will be given to you." You MUST ask your clients for referrals.

Here are four ways that you can do it.

1. Let Them Know that Other Clients Refer

Put up a notice board in a prominent place in your waiting room showing the clients that have made referrals in the last month. Mimic it on your Website and in your monthly newsletter. It will send the message that you expect clients to refer.

2. Run Referral Promotions

Referral promotions can take the form of competition in which current clients get coupons, cards, or certificates they can endorse, like a check, to give out to other pet owners. These recipients can then bring them back into the practice to be redeemed for a discount, a free gift, or (preferably) a free upgrade to a premium service with their first appointment. Prizes are awarded to the client(s) responsible for the most referrals during the contest.

Make sure that you offer prizes that are worth the effort or it won't work. Obviously, you will be able to afford better and more expensive prizes if you run the competition over a longer period.

For example, how many new referrals would you need to get before you could afford to give away a free widescreen TV? Not that many, actually, but the perceived value to your clients is huge. You would expect that the winner of your referral competition would make more than one referral, so even though a widescreen TV seems like an expensive item to give away, when you compare it to the average value of a client, it really isn't.

Another thing to bear in mind is that these kinds of competition will create a buzz about your practice among your team and your clients, in itself a huge value to your marketing program.

3. Hold Referral Events

If you want to meet a lot of potential clients at once, hold a special event for your clients and invite them to bring their pet-owning friends. Make sure that you provide entertainment, a buffet, and drinks for maximum effect. You want to make a big impact with your potential new clients, so push the boat out for them. If you get dozens of clients to bring along dozens of potential clients, you will get back way more than the cost of the event.

4. Ask Why They Don't Refer

This last tactic takes a little bit of courage and a strong relationship. Nevertheless, if a pet owner has been coming to your practice for years but never makes a referral, you need to ask why. (Of course, you can only do this if you keep records of your referrals.)

At the end of the next appointment, ask if you can speak candidly for a moment. (A client detained unwillingly is not a good source of information.) If consent is granted, ask whether you are providing good service. Since this is a long-term client, the expected answer is, "Yes." Now point out that you noticed from the records that there haven't been any referrals and ask for an explanation that can help you understand that.

Explain the benefits of referring another pet owner. This may be new information. If it is, then it will alert you to another area you need to work on—making sure clients know rewards are offered for referrals. When you get an explanation, take it seriously. No one likes to be asked for advice, give it, and then be ignored.

Golden Referral Key #3

Reward Them!

We mentioned earlier about conditioning your clients to refer. Rewarding them plays a key role in the conditioning process.

As you may know, we are based just north of Orlando, and SeaWorld is therefore a frequent destination to take our kids. If you go to see the Shamu Show, you will notice that each time the giant killer whale or one of his pals performs a trick, he is rewarded with some tasty fish.

Over time the whales have been conditioned to do as their trainers ask so that they will be rewarded. Eventually, doing the tricks becomes second nature. You need to discover what is the "fish" that will condition your clients to refer so that they will be rewarded. You want referring to become second nature to them.

You must make referrals a big deal and, at the very least, call your client to say thank you for the referral or send a thank you note and/or gift.

Do you think that if one of your clients received a nice thank you card, with perhaps a gift certificate, for making a referral that they would be more likely to refer someone else?

You bet they would!

Not only that, but how many people would get to know that they'd received a thank you from their vet?

A really good way to promote a referral reward scheme to is

to offer a choice of gifts in return for referring another client to your practice. We have found that the best three choices are a pet product that you currently sell in your practice up to the value of about $50, a free dental exam up to a value of about $50, and a $25 gift certificate to a local restaurant.

(Usually more people will request the restaurant certificate than the other two gifts combined, even though they have a higher value.)

Once you have established what your three gift choices will be, the next step is to have some large signs strategically placed in your waiting room that convey this offer. Below the sign, display a sample of each gift.

Golden Referral Key #4

Track Them!

Referral programs only work if you keep an accurate record of who has referred whom. This is important for two reasons:

1. The quickest way to turn a client's trust to alienation is to neglect to provide the reward you have promised for referring a new client.

2. The only way you will know how your referral program is working is to track the number of referrals you are receiving each month. We recommend setting monthly referral targets and putting a member of your team in charge of keeping score.

Referrals Don't Just Happen, You Must Work for Them!

If you need more new clients and you're not consistently getting a flood of referrals, then it is most likely due to one or more of the following reasons:

1. You haven't created an experience that your clients feel compelled to tell others about.

2. You haven't developed an effective referral program.

3. You haven't enlisted enough team support: either they don't have enough incentive or they don't understand the importance of referrals.

Put these right and your referrals will be healthy.

We cannot emphasize enough how important referrals are to the growth of your practice in the New Economy. The good news is that no matter how many referrals you are already enjoying, you can work as a practice to get more.

If you implement nothing else in this book, implement a referral program, then sit back and watch your referrals soar!

CHAPTER 13
TESTIMONIALS—ENHANCING YOUR POSITION WITH SOCIAL PROOF

Be everywhere, do everything, and never fail to astonish the customer.

–Macy's Motto

One of the most powerful tools you can use to enhance your client attraction strategies are testimonials.

Why Use Testimonials?

In today's world, people are subjected constantly to so much advertising hype that we have become a nation of skeptics. Put simply, people are so sick of being deceived that they find it hard to trust or believe any claims that are made by any businesses.

For example, probably every veterinary practice in your area, including yours, claims to be the most caring and friendly, but only one can be telling the truth, so why should your prospective clients believe you?

What they require is proof, and the best form of proof a veterinary practice can offer is the testimonial of a happy and satisfied client.

You see…

When you make a statement about how good your practice is, it's a claim; but when one of your clients makes the same statement, it's a fact!

Anatomy of a Good Testimonial

The key to a good testimonial is that it gets your message across and it is believable.

One of the best ways to convey your message is by using what we call a Before & After Testimonial.

The Before is the problem or dissatisfaction that brought the client to you, and the After is the solution and satisfaction that you provided. These work particularly well because the problem or dissatisfaction your client was experiencing before coming to you is the same problem or dissatisfaction your prospective clients are experiencing right now.

A good example of a Before & After Testimonial is this one:

> *We got sick and tired of being taken for granted by our previous vet, so when a friend told us about the service and care she and her cats got from XYZ Veterinary Clinic, we jumped at the chance to see for ourselves. We booked an appointment for Penny, our Persian cat, and have been amazed at the high quality of service and care. We definitely recommend any cat owner to give them a try. You won't regret it!*
>
> **Debbie Smith** (Penny's Mom),
> Sanford, FL

Here's one highlighting the quality of patient care:

> *Our 4 year old Black Lab, Bonnie, suffered with skin problems since she was a puppy and nothing seemed to work until we changed our vets to XYZ Veterinary Clinic. On our very first visit they were able to identify a problem our previous vets couldn't and now Bonnie has a healthy skin and is happier for it.*
>
> **John Brown (owner of Bonnie)**,
> Heathrow, FL
> November 23rd, 2010

Another strategy is to use a testimonial either to back up a claim you are making or to allay a doubt or fear that a potential client may have about coming to your practice.

For example, suppose your marketing makes a claim that you're "on time every time." A good testimonial for this would be:

> *I'm a mom and also run my own business from home so I can't afford for appointments to run late, which is why I love XYZ Veterinary Clinic. I've been bringing Dudley & Margo, our Miniature Dachshunds, here for four years and they've never been late yet!*
>
> **Emma Fletcher** (Dudley & Margo's Mom),
> Lake Mary, FL

If the cost of your services is an issue for some prospects (which it should be, by the way; you never want to have the lowest rates in your market) then this could be a good testimonial:

> *I live 30 miles away from XYZ Veterinary Clinic but I drive past at least 30 other veterinary practices to get here! They may not be the cheapest vets around but the service and care they provide is the best in the area and I wouldn't take my dogs anywhere else.*
>
> **Bill Jones**,
> Orlando, FL

This testimonial is a double endorsement because it implies how good the clinic must be to justify the distance travelled, even for a premium price.

No doubt you have your own examples of getting your message across with testimonials, but how do you make them believable? In other words, even though the client is telling the truth, what can you do to make a prospective client believe it?

Well, first of all you need to convince them that the testimonial came from a real person and wasn't just something you made up. The best way to do this is to provide the testimonial giver's first and last names (and the pet's name), along with the city and state. This can be made even more credible by adding a date to the testimonial. Best of all, if possible, include a photograph of the client and pet.

Combine all of those elements, and you've got yourself a pretty compelling testimonial!

How to Get Testimonials from Your Clients

The quick answer is to ask them!

Start by targeting long-time clients who have a good relationship with you. Ask them if they are willing to share their good experiences with others.

Another technique is to train your veterinarians or veterinary nurses or technicians to ask for a testimonial from clients who are obviously happy with the care their pet has just received.

Remember to give your clients compelling reasons why you are asking them. Two such reasons are that they will be helping other pet owners make the right decision for their pets and that they will be doing the practice a favor. (It feels good to be able to do a favor for another person, especially one who has been helpful.)

There are three key times when asking for testimonials comes naturally:

1. **At the end of the first new-patient appointment**

   There's an old saying that first impressions count. If you cannot impress a client whose pet you are seeing for the first time, then you've got serious problems that testimonials won't solve.

   We hope instead that you will have been able to create a strongly favorable impression by the friendly and efficient way your team arranged the appointment, made your client welcome upon arrival, and saw to their comfort during (ideally) the brief wait before seeing a veterinarian. If you haven't found anything wrong with the pet, there should be nothing but smiles at the experience you have created.

   This makes it the perfect time to ask for initial impressions of your practice and of the entire experience. You'd like to hear what a wonderful experience it was and (if you're lucky) how much better you are than the last vet who saw the pet!

Once you have gotten to this point, asking for a testimonial is easy.

2. **At the pet's annual checkup.**

As with a new-patient appointment, if you have given a pet owner the thumbs-up that everything is fine with Rover since his last visit, your client is likely to be smiling if only in relief!

So ask about the visit and any observations about the practice generally. At the strategic moment, ask for a testimonial and, if agreeable, arrange for it to be given.

One thing to note here is that these should not be long drawn out conversations. You just want to make sure your client is disposed to approve, ask for a testimonial, and then hand off to a team member who can take the statement.

The type of testimonials you are looking for here is your clients' statements they have been coming for years and always been pleased or that they always bring their pets to you and wouldn't dream of going anywhere else.

3. **At the end of the final appointment after a successful course of treatment.**

The other time when a client is likely to be smiling is when you have successfully treated a pet, especially if it was for a serious or life-threatening condition.

In these instances, you are looking for testimonials that give social proof that you are indeed an expert in your field. For example, if the owner of a dog with a skin problem reads how you were able to treat successfully a dog with a similar problem, it will create confidence you can do the same for her dog.

How and Where to Use Testimonials

Understanding why you should use testimonials and what makes a good one, you're ready to consider how you use them in your practice.

There are four ways to use testimonials in your practice, and we'll talk about them in order of effectiveness with the most effective first:

Live Testimonials

There is nothing more powerful than having one of your clients telling your prospects face-to-face how good your practice is and why they should join. The way to accomplish this is to hold a live event, such as a fun day or open evening, to which you invite local pet owners. The other way to do this is to hold a client appreciation event and ask your clients to bring their pet-owning friends.

The next step is to identify 5 or more clients who would be happy to give a testimonial in front of the guests at the event. Once the event is in full swing, you simply ask for everyone's attention, say a few words of welcome and introduction, and then invite your chosen clients to say what they have to say.

Video Testimonials

The next most powerful testimonial, and one that can be used again and again, is a video testimonial.

Video testimonials can be collected in two ways. First, you should have a video camera in your practice that can be used to record testimonials from happy clients when they bring their pets in for their appointments. The video testimonial should contain all the elements we discussed earlier that constitute the anatomy of a testimonial. It is important that you coach the client on how to give a testimonial. The alternative is to ask questions off camera that prompt the responses you want.

We recommend that you use the Kodak Zi8 Pocket Video Camera, a low-cost but exceptionally high-quality pocket-sized High Definition video camera. We use it ourselves for all our video recording, and we believe it is the best camera value on the market.

Providing you've got plenty of happy clients (and they're not too camera shy!), you should be able to collect several video testimonials during a week.

The other way to collect video testimonials is at a client appreciation or other live event such as those described earlier. You can then get lots of happy clients on camera in one afternoon or evening!

Using Your Video Testimonials

There are three really effective ways to use your video testimonials:

1. **On Your Website**

As we described earlier, most veterinarians do not use their Websites effectively, and the visitors to most veterinary Websites therefore leave almost as soon as they arrive. But imagine visitors to your Website finding dozens of videos showing raving fans of your practice telling them how wonderful it is to be a client and why.

Do you think they would be more inclined to bring their pets to your practice than to the practice with the bland-brochure site? Of course they would! Testimonials have a magnetic effect: when people see other people having a good experience, they naturally want that same experience for themselves. So when a prospective client sees client after client raving about how great your practice is, they feel left out and want to become part of it. That's the power of video testimonials.

The good news is that with the advent of video hosting sites such as YouTube.com, it is very easy to put videos on your Website. You can have a video testimonial on your Website within minutes of recording it.

2. On TV in Your Reception/Waiting Area

Putting a TV on the wall of your practice's reception area is a great idea, because it allows you to deliver your marketing messages directly to the people who are most likely to spend money with you, your current clients! Using video testimonials inside your practice is a really powerful strategy because it reassures your clients that they are bringing their pets to the best there is. It must be the best if all of these other people are saying so, right?

It also boosts a client's ego to be one of the clients in the video, as you are effectively making that client a celebrity. But most importantly it teaches your clients that they are expected to give testimonials, and they will be more forthcoming when it's their turn.

3. On a DVD

A great marketing strategy is to produce a DVD that includes a message from you, a tour of your practice, and some video testimonials. This DVD can then be sent to prospective clients, given to current clients to share with other pet owners they know, and supplied to other related businesses (such as independent pet shops) to pass along to their clients.

It also makes an excellent gift to put into a "Shock & Awe" box (see Chapter 23), especially if the DVD also contains a tour of the practice and interviews with your veterinarians.

Photo Testimonials

The third most powerful form of testimonial is a photograph. Everyone has heard that a picture is worth a thousand words. Well, there are no better pictures than those of you or your staff posing with happy clients and their pets. Here are three places you can use those "happy snaps":

1. Testimonial Book

Imagine having a book entitled *The Happy Pets of XYZ Practice* containing photos of happy clients with their pets, accompanied by a testimonial from each client.

Now imagine the impact of giving this book to new clients and sending it out to prospective clients. Do you think that they might want to have the same experience as the pet owners in the book? Of course they would!

And if you give a copy of the book to each of the clients in it, do you think they might show it to their friends and family? You bet they will!

It shouldn't cost a lot to produce such a book. If you do it in letter size, folded in half, with a glossy cardboard cover, it will look great and be very effective.

2. Photo Wall

Another great way to use photo testimonials is a photo wall. Clear one of the walls in your reception area (somewhere that will be noticed by clients...behind the reception desk is ideal) and stick up photos of smiling clients with their pets.

Another tip for a photo wall is to be clever about the placement of the photos. Try to stick photos of friends and family next to each other and, if a client's pet dies, put their photo with any new pet next to the old one. This not only creates a strong bond with the client but shows new clients that people keep faith with you through the life of every pet they own.

3. To Enhance Written Testimonials

In a moment we'll tell you about the places you can use written testimonials, but as a rule of thumb any written testimonial will be viewed as much more credible if it has a photo of the client with it.

4. On Your Website

If you can't get a video testimonial, put photos on your Website instead. You can also use your happy client photos on your social media pages such as Facebook and Flickr.

Written Testimonials

While this last form of testimonial is the least effective, using it is still many times more beneficial to the growth of your practice than not using testimonials at all. Written testimonials include both testimony written by your client and transcriptions of oral testimony they gave in person or on video.

There are four main places we recommend that you use written testimonials for maximum benefit and effect. Be sure to use all of them.

1. In Direct Mail Pieces

Testimonials should be used to add credibility to your

marketing message as an essential part of any marketing letter or postcard you mail.

2. On Newspaper/Magazine Advertisements

New prospects are more likely to respond to newspaper, magazine, or even Yellow Pages ads when a testimonial is included.

3. In Your Newsletter

Your monthly newsletter is a great place to put testimonials. It trains your clients that you expect them and reassures them that they're with the right vets. It is also gives great kudos to the client giving the testimonial.

4. On Your Website

If you can't get a video testimonial to put on your Website, then use a written one. Remember any form of testimonial is better than none. Very few veterinary practices put testimonials on their Websites, so even a written testimonial will set your Website apart from those of your competitors.

The Celebrity Testimonial

One type of testimonial carries much more weight than others, and that is a testimonial from a celebrity. Let's face it, everyone likes to be associated with celebrities, which explains why companies such as Coca-Cola® and Pepsi® spend millions of dollars each year on celebrity endorsements.

So where can you find a celebrity to say nice things about your veterinary practice? There are basically three types of celebrity available to your practice. Here's where you'll find them:

The Current Celebrity Client

Depending on the size of your practice and your location, a local celebrity's pet may already attend your practice, although you might not know it. If you're lucky enough to have Carrie Underwood's dog as a patient, great. Otherwise, remember that there are different levels of celebrity, and all we really mean by the term is someone who is recognized, respected, and liked.

That could be your local Mayor, TV news anchor or weather forecaster, or radio host; a professional golfer or college football player; or even someone who appeared on TV auditioning for American Idol!

You may have to do some detective work to establish who your celebrity clients are because, depending on how well known they are, there's a good chance they won't actually brings their pets to the practice themselves. But it will be more than worth the effort to find out who they are.

If you do have a celebrity client, don't be afraid to ask for a testimonial. Remember, people like to return favors, and celebrities are people!

The Local Celebrity Pet Owner

If you don't have any celebrity clients, then find one! You'll be surprised at how little you have to invest to get a celebrity to endorse your practice. (Complimentary care for their pet could be an inducement). Whenever you hear about a local celebrity's pet, make a note to reach out and follow up.

For example, we've noticed a lot of car dealers using their dogs in TV commercials. You could offer to give a dog complimentary care in return for some publicity by the car dealer. You could make this work even better by getting the car dealer to give special-offer vouchers for your practice to every person who purchased a car. In doing this, you are leveraging the car dealer's customers to get your practice more clients.

The Local Hero

If you can't get a TV or sports celebrity then try a local hero. The local firefighter who has just been in the news for saving a family or the police officer who caught a bad guy or a local pet owner serving in the armed forces are all good candidates.

So do your practice a favor and go grab a celebrity!

SECTION 3

CLIENT RETENTION

Putting a Fence around Your Clients:
How to keep your clients happy, engaged, and resistant to approaches from other practices.

CHAPTER 14
THE FATAL ASSUMPTION

Customer satisfaction is worthless. Customer loyalty is priceless.

–Jeffrey Gitomer

The second Pillar of Veterinary Practice Growth is client retention. Most veterinarians assume that if a client brought her pet in for a wellness exam today, she will naturally return in twelve months time.

Making this assumption can be a costly mistake. Twelve months could just as easily be a lifetime, and a lot of water can pass under the bridge during those twelve months.

You might think that your clients are thinking about your practice between annual visits and are out there telling all of their friends how great you are. The reality is a little different! People have a lot on their minds and a lot going on in their lives. In most cases, they are not thinking of your practice when they're not there, and you're not in a pet-owner's mind until the pet needs to see you, which for many will be just once a year. While this is not necessarily a reason for clients to leave your practice, it's not a reason to stay either.

You need to take your practice from an out-of-sight/out-of-mind relationship with your clients to an ever-present, top-of-consciousness position. We'll show you exactly how you can do this, just as soon as we look at some of the reasons clients do leave your practice.

Why Clients Leave

At the beginning of this book, we observed that as of the end of 2010, visits to veterinary practices were down at least 6% over the previous twelve months. The economy was partly to blame, but other reasons also explain why pet owners leave veterinary practices. The good news is that there are ways to address all of these reasons, including the economic ones.

Sure, some pet owners have stopped visiting veterinary practices. However, others have just left yours. They have chosen to move to another veterinary practice. The most successful veterinary practices are actually gaining clients, and you can too! Starting with the obvious, here are four reasons why clients could be leaving your practice.

Economic Challenges

It's a sad fact of life that people are facing economic challenges, and your clients who have seen a drop in their disposable incomes may have stopped coming in simply because their finances dictate that they can't.

A common reaction to this is to think about reducing your fees, but this is a huge mistake—it's a war you can't win. A better solution is to target more affluent clients. Pet owners with larger disposable incomes are still spending money on their pets and not just on essentials such as health.

We recently paid a visit to a local designer pet store selling such items as Halloween costumes and designer clothing for dogs, as well as all other manner of pet-related gifts and accessories. Not only was the shop busy but pet owners were quite happily paying $40 and up for designer dog bowls!

There are shops like this all over the country, not to mention the online stores. The pet owners buying from these shops are taking their pets to someone for their healthcare needs. Why shouldn't it be to you?

Relocation

When clients leave the area, taking their pets with them, there's not much you can do about it. Or is there?

We know a veterinary practice in Orlando with a client that drives all the way from Kentucky for their dog's annual checkup! While that's an extreme example, there are many other clients still in this practice who have moved shorter distances but to locations that would still be considered outside of their catchment area. These clients could choose to visit any of several other veterinary clinics closer to home, but they don't.

If you are different and give your clients an experience and level of patient care they can't get somewhere else, then if they can afford it, they will travel from pretty much anywhere to get it. On the other hand, if you provide ordinary service and the same experience as every other veterinary practice, then your clients won't have any trouble finding the same thing in their new locations!

Dissatisfaction

Dissatisfaction might not be the right word here because, let's get one thing straight, if all you are doing is satisfying your clients then there is a very good chance that they will be tempted to go elsewhere.

Your veterinary business is not just about treating pets but about your relationship with your clients. If you take them for granted, just seek to satisfy their expectations or worse, leave them feeling unsatisfied with your service, then they are vulnerable to seduction by a competitor practice waving some shiny new object (e.g. a new service, new piece of equipment, or new experience) in front of them.

They Get A Better Offer!

Another thing happening during those twelve long months is that your competitors are actively targeting your clients! Remember, a veterinarian is who is better at marketing will have more success than one that is more clinically skilled.

Being a great veterinarian does not automatically mean you will attract and keep more clients than less talented veterinarians. Your clients and prospects can only judge by what they are told and what they experience for themselves. Clients can have short memories, and if your competitors are constantly telling them that there is more to offer at another practice, then eventually that message will get through.

New practices with newer facilities that open near your clients, perhaps even closer to their homes than your practice is, are certainly a threat, especially if they offer incentives to try something new.

Even established practices, though, if they're on their game, will use any excuse to reach out to your clients. They will be only too pleased to brag about their new equipment, their newly refurbished facilities, or their new veterinarian's reputation.

CHAPTER 15
ENGAGING WITH YOUR CLIENTS

You can have everything in life that you want
if you just give enough other people what they want.

–Zig Ziglar

To prevent your clients from leaving, you need to put an iron cage around them, metaphorically speaking. One of our mentors, marketing legend Dan Kennedy, teaches business owners to think of themselves as ranchers assembling and caring for herds of good, responsive customers.

The rancher's biggest job is to put a fence around his herd so that they don't escape and wander off to pastures new!

The question you must ask yourself as a veterinary practice owner is this:

How do I build a fence around my clients
and how do I maintain it?

Building Your Fence

Fundamentally, people make decisions based on pain or pleasure. They do something either because of the pain that will result from not doing it or because of the pleasure that will come from doing it. For your clients, your fence has to evoke pleasure in staying with your practice and invoke pain at disconnecting from you.

In other words, you have to create an environment where your clients are happy to belong and which they're reluctant to leave, based on the quality and perceived value of your service, the friendliness of your staff, and the WOW Factor, all of which combine to make you unique.

Once you begin to create this environment (perhaps your practice has it already?), the critical task for maintaining your fence (i.e. keeping your clients) is:

Frequent Quality Communication!

Your clients must be reminded constantly of their membership in your herd and of the associated benefits, so that they are not tempted to stray elsewhere.

What is Quality Communication?

Quality communication is communicating with your clients in way that is of benefit to them. The four main ways you can do this are:

1. Educate Them

Teach them about preventative healthcare for their pets. For example show them how to clean their dogs teeth and the dangers of feeding candy to their dogs. They'll be grateful that you have their pets best interests at heart and that you are helping them to avoid large veterinary bills.

2. Entertain Them

Share funny stories, photos and videos from your practice and about pets in general. Give them something to smile about! They'll be grateful you brightened their day.

3. Reward Them

Send them goodies for referring, or because it's their birthday, or just because they chose you as their veterinarian. They'll love the fact that you care and they'll tell their friends too.

4. Compel Them

Make them compelling offers that will be of benefit to them and their pets such as special promotions and offers on food etc. They'll be grateful that you're helping them out and they'll spend more money in your practice!

How often is frequent?

We recommend at least weekly communication with clients. This may sound like a lot but it isn't, considering that some of these communications are by e-mail and automated.

Your fence-maintaining communications need to encompass the following areas:

1. Holidays & Celebrations

All clients should receive greetings or gifts to commemorate such events as:

- Thanksgiving
- Christmas

- Hanukkah
- Pet's Birthday
- Client's Birthday
- Anniversary of first visit

Other holidays that can also serve as an occasion for getting in touch are:

- Halloween
- St Patrick's Day
- New Year's Day
- Independence Day

Note: you do not have to send something at every holiday and anniversary but just be aware that they are all good excuses to send a marketing message. As a rule of thumb it is always a good idea to give your clients a good reason as to why you are sending them something whether it be information or an offer.

2. Client Event Promotions

Every practice worth its salt should hold at least one client appreciation event every year as a way to thank clients for their support. You should mail personal invitations to these annual events and then follow up with e-mail reminders.

These events should be memorable, with food, drinks, and even entertainment. Make sure you get someone to photograph the whole thing so that you can use the photos in your marketing. Video-recording parts of the event is a good idea, as you can use it to show prospective clients what they are missing out on and that you really take care of your clients.

3. Weekly E-mail

Almost everyone has, or has access to, a device for sending and receiving e-mails, whether it be a computer or some variety of handheld device. It is now possible, for a small monthly fee, to get access to online auto responder services that can send e-mails automatically to your clients at pre-scheduled times.

This means you can write e-mails in advance, to be delivered each week on autopilot. By giving your clients useful information about how to care for their pets or how to spot various ailments, you can keep in touch, provide value, and encourage more visits.

4. Websites & Social Media

We recommend that every veterinary practice have a blog on its Website for two reasons.

The first is because it is the easiest and quickest way to build your Website, a key criterion for Google ranking.

The second is because it allows you another way to connect with your clients. Letting your clients know of interesting things that are going on in your practice and in your personal/family life will help them to develop a rapport with you.

As we observed in the chapter on Internet Marketing, social media Websites such as Facebook and Twitter are playing an ever greater role in connecting with your clients. With nearly 50% of Americans now on Facebook, it has become an essential tool for any veterinary practice. If you're not a Facebook user yourself, at least half your team probably are! Delegate to one of them the responsibility for your Facebook fan page.

5. Monthly Newsletters

The single biggest thing you can do to maintain your fence is to produce and mail a monthly newsletter to your clients.

Why?

Because it is a tangible publication that they receive in their mailbox every month and, if done properly, your clients will actually look forward to receiving it.

Another benefit is that it guarantees that you will keep in touch with your clients while building yet more rapport with them by providing useful and amusing content.

The other thing to bear in mind is that any sort of positive media exposure you put out—whether it be in print in a book or client newsletter, a TV appearance, or a local radio interview—will strengthen your reputation and positioning as the local animal health expert.

Our advice is to start building your fence today, before your heard strays into the corral of another veterinary practice!

CHAPTER 16
HOW TO MAKE CLIENT NEWSLETTERS WORK

It is the service we are not obliged to give that people value most.

–J. C. Penney, 1934

The single biggest thing you can do to maintain a relationship with your clients, so that they feel like they belong to your practice and do not think about straying elsewhere, is to produce and mail out a monthly newsletter.

A newsletter not only provides relationship value but properly done, it will pull in appointments that you would not have had otherwise.

This chapter will tell you how you do it properly.

1. It Must Be a Printed Newsletter (Not E-mail!)

Although it is possible and very popular to send out digital newsletters, e-mail does not have the same impact or perceived value as printed newsletters. With a printed newsletter, you increase impact by engaging your clients' other senses—the touch of the newsletter, the sound of its opening, the smell of the ink and paper.

You also improve its ability to get attention. Your clients receive dozens of e-mails each day, and even if your newsletter e-mail didn't end up in their junk folder, there is a good chance it would be deleted unread. If the e-mail newsletter went to a computer used for work, even the client who wanted to read it wouldn't have time to read all of it.

A printed newsletter that comes in the mail, on the other hand, can be read at leisure and passed along to friends or family for yet further exposure.

2. It Must Be Delivered Every Month

It has been proven in a whole host of different industries that bi-monthly and quarterly newsletters just don't work, period. Sixty or ninety days is just too long to leave your herd unattended. In the long intervals between newsletters, too many could have moved to other pastures.

A monthly publication gives you the chance more frequently to reinforce your sales message, thank your clients for referrals, and remind them that you're there and ready to serve them.

3. It Must Be Personal

One of the most important reasons to do a newsletter is to connect with your clients, to help maintain a bond that they will find hard to break. You do this by making it personal to them and by sharing the personalities and stories of your practice with them. This makes your relationship with them much less formal, creating trust and friendlier perception of your practice.

Making It Personal To Your Client

With the advent of variable data printing, it is now extremely easy to personalize your newsletters to a high degree. For example, in the newsletters we produce for our clients, we use each veterinary client's first name in several places, as well as name of that client's animal. We also put a photo of the animal's breed on the front of the newsletter, and might even use a photo of the actual pet (if we have a picture that is of decent quality).

We include referral vouchers that have the client's name on them, which they can give out to their pet-owning friends who receive incentives for joining the practice. Of course, because the vouchers have the referring clients' names on them, it makes it very easy to track where referrals have come from.

Receiving a personalized newsletter every month with a pet's photo on the front creates a strong connection and is definitely something our clients would miss if they moved to another practice.

Another way to personalize it and really cater to your best clients is to include a Pet of the Month feature that includes a photograph and a testimonial from the pet owner. The pet owner will be delighted to showcase the pet and to show the newsletter to anyone who will look at it. This feature encourages other pet owners to send in photos of their pets with their own testimonials, which can be used not only in newsletters but in other areas of your practice where testimonials are important, as described in Chapter 9.

We actually know veterinary practices that have waiting lists of clients who want their pets featured as Pet of the Month! They have clients lining up essentially to give them testimonials so they can see their pets in the newsletter.

How many clients do you have lining up to give you testimonials?

Making It Personal To You And Your Practice

Most of your clients may only see you once a year, so injecting your personality into your newsletter is extremely important to sustaining your connection with them.

We recommend three ways to make your newsletter all yours. First, include a photo of you and your partner(s) and associates on the front of the newsletter with a small article offering your reflections for the month. This will help your clients know you better and feel that you know them.

Second, have a Team Member of the Month feature that includes a photo and a short bio—marital status and children, pets, likes/dislikes, hobbies, community activities, education and training, and why they like working with animals. This will reassure your clients that you have competent staff who are friendly, interesting, approachable pet owners and good citizens, just like them! It will also make them feel more comfortable when they visit your practice as they will recognize your team members from the newsletter.

Last, include an article written by a pet personality within your practice. Publish an article in each newsletter that seems to have been written by your practice's resident pet, your own animal, or the pet of a team member. Your clients will not only love reading this but will want to share their own stories.

4. It Must Be Entertaining & Interesting

When your newsletter arrives each month, you want it to be a welcome guest not an unwelcome pest, so it must have something inside that will make recipients want to read it. All the foregoing advice about personalizing your newsletter is important for interest and entertainment as well. The newsletters that work best for clients also contain games, trivia, quizzes, and celebrity news.

Provide helpful information, too, such as hints and tips on pet care and even information that is not pet-related, such as general health.

5. It Must Contain An Offer

Your newsletter is an opportunity you can't afford to pass up, to offer your clients an inducement to come into your practice and spend money.

This inducement could be a discounted service, a premium for booking an appointment, or a special offer on food. Ask your local pet food and pharmaceutical sales representatives what they have that you can offer in your newsletter. The idea is to ethically entice your clients to visit your practice when they wouldn't necessarily have done so otherwise.

Figure 10 shows the front page of an actual newsletter we developed for a client in Longwood, Florida. We have changed the recipient identification details but the rest of the newsletter is actual content.

As you can see, the client's name (Mike) is used in several places, and the photograph shows Mike's breed of dog, an Airedale Terrier, and actually references the pet by name in the text next to the photograph.

The bottom half of the front page includes a message from the practice owner together with his photo, in a pet-friendly pose.

Notice there are also three referral vouchers personalized with the client's name. In this case the vouchers entitle the recipient to $25 gift card for a local restaurant on their first new-client appointment just for being a friend of the person who referred them.

Putting these referral vouchers in the newsletter each month is really important for at least three reasons.

LVC
LONGWOOD
VETERINARY CLINIC

Mike,
Let's Talk
PET TALK

Visit us online at www.LongwoodVet.com (407) 834-2526

Longwood Veterinary Clinic • 1080 W State Road 434 • Longwood, FL 32750

Mike...
Your
December 2010
Newsletter

PRESORTED
FIRST-CLASS MAIL
U.S. POSTAGE
PAID
TAMPA, FL
PERMIT #2245

Here is your Monthly Newsletter from your friends at Longwood Veterinary Clinic. We look forward to seeing you and Zeke the next time you pay us a visit. Don't be a stranger... prevention is much better than treatment for your pet and your pocket book! Look out for the great offers we have for you this month!
And remember when you visit us... **seeing YOUR pet is THE most important part of our day!**

**** 3-DIGIT 327 6/1 ****
Mike Smith
950 Newcastle Road
Lake Mary, FL 32746-7163

Mike, Look On The Back Of This Newsletter For This Month's EXCITING NEW OFFERS!

Dear Mike,

The holiday season is once again here; bringing food, family, and fun for both you and your pet. The season also brings a change in the weather. We may not get snow here in Florida, but the cooler weather can affect our pets. This month's article focuses on arthritis, a condition that can be aggravated by the cooler temperatures.

If you think your pet may be suffering from arthritis, be sure to take advantage of this month's exclusive client offer. When you bring your pet in for an orthopedic exam, you will receive 25% off any initial treatment your vet prescribes, including anti-inflammatories, alternative therapies, and prescription diets. Don't forget about our referral rewards program! Every time you refer a new pet owner to our clinic using the vouchers below, you will be rewarded with a $25 gift card for BoneFish Grill. The person you refer will get one too!

Happy Holidays to you, your pets, and your family!

Dr Rick Marrinson, Owner
Longwood Veterinary Clinic

LONGWOOD
VETERINARY CLINIC
"Care To Share" Program
As a friend of
Mike Smith
This coupon entitles me to a $25.00 gift card for **Bonefish Grill** after my first new patient appointment.
Appointment must be paid in full to qualify.

LONGWOOD
VETERINARY CLINIC
"Care To Share" Program
As a friend of
Mike Smith
This coupon entitles me to a $25.00 gift card for **Bonefish Grill** after my first new patient appointment.
Appointment must be paid in full to qualify.

LONGWOOD
VETERINARY CLINIC
"Care To Share" Program
As a friend of
Mike Smith
This coupon entitles me to a $25.00 gift card for **Bonefish Grill** after my first new patient appointment.
Appointment must be paid in full to qualify.

Figure 10 - Example of A Client Newsletter

First, it makes it very easy for your clients to refer their friends and family. After all, if your friend or family member is looking for a veterinary clinic, it makes you feel good to be able to help them out, and they're going to feel good about you if they get their problem solved and also get a $25 gift card as a result of your recommendation.

Second, there is a good chance that sometime during the year your client will get the opportunity to refer, even if not proactively. Because the vouchers are in the newsletter each month, you are almost guaranteeing that whenever the opportunity arises, your client will be more than eager to use one.

Finally, the inclusion of the vouchers each month will help train your clients that they are expected to refer. To back this up we also suggest that you include a list of people who referred the previous month. This sends the message to your clients that other people are referring and are being rewarded for their efforts.

Getting Your Newsletter Out

To get your newsletter out each month you need to decide what it is going to look like and whether you are going to produce it in house or via a third party.

The newsletter shown in figure 10 is printed at a professional printing company in color on glossy 17" by 10" paper which is then folded in half in booklet style. The newsletter is then folded in half again and tabbed for mailing. This gives it a really nice look and feel but it doesn't have to be as fancy as this. A black and white newsletter printed on plain paper is better than no newsletter at all!

Getting it printed and mailed from a printers has the benefit that you just have to concentrate on putting the content together and they can do the labor intensive part. They will also be able to do some fancy things that you can't such as variable data printing so that you can make it highly personalized to your clients and their pets. You do need, however, to give the printers a good idea of what you want it to look like and be able to provide them with your client data in the correct format they need to merge the data correctly.

If you are going to produce your newsletter in house then the quickest and cheapest way is to produce the same newsletter for every client and then mail them in envelopes with mailing labels printed from your practice management system. They are not likely to be as effective as the personalized newsletters but they will 100% more effective than not sending one.

The alternative to producing the newsletter in house or dealing with a printer directly is to use a managed service such as our Easy4Vets™ 'Done For You' service (see Resources for the Website address.) Because we publish newsletters for a number of veterinary practices we have been able to negotiate extremely competitive rates with a printing company who specialize in variable data printing. We are also able to convert your client data into the format they need and provide breed images for each breed of dog and cat.

Whichever way you choose to produce your newsletter, make it the responsibility of someone in your practice to ensure it gets out **every** month so that it is something your clients get used to receiving on a regular basis and look forward to arriving in their mailbox.

CHAPTER 17
STOPPING THE LEAKS BEFORE THEY START

Every contact we have with a customer influences whether or not they'll come back. We have to be great every time or we'll lose them.

–Kevin Stirtz
Author of *More Loyal Customers: 21 Real World Lessons to Keep Your Customers Coming Back*

A Note about Scheduling Appointments and Reminders

We see two big client retention problems arising from the way most veterinary practices manage annual appointments.

The first is that they don't schedule the next appointment while the client is still on the premises at the end of the current appointment.

When you allow your client to leave the building without scheduling the next appointment, you are effectively sending the message that this was a one-off transaction and, although you hope for a return in twelve months, you don't have any expectations.

Now think about what happens when you visit a good dentist. The last thing they do before you leave the premises is to give you a card or printout showing your next appointment date on it. A similar thing happens when you visit the barber or hairdresser.

It doesn't really matter if you don't know your schedule twelve months in advance or whether the client can plan a year in advance. The point is that by giving an appointment you are getting a commitment. An appointment can always be changed if the date becomes a problem, and this should be presented as a positive for the client. You explain that appointments go really quickly and that scheduling now secures a spot for next year, and most clients are only too happy to go along.

The second problem we see in the management of annual appointments is the reminder process. Most veterinary practices send out the first reminder about two weeks before the appointment date, usually by e-mail. The next reminder is probably mailed after the appointment was missed, and a phone call might follow a few days or weeks after that. Your practice may vary the details but the sequence may be similar.

The first problem with this sequence is that if you didn't schedule an appointment during their previous visit, and then you just give a couple of weeks notice about the next one, there's a chance the appointment can't be kept and your former client may be tempted to go elsewhere if that hasn't already happened.

It's much harder to get a client back if you don't notice the absence until it's too late. There is a place for sending out reminders, but don't underestimate the power of making the call first.

Use the Telephone Proactively Rather Than Reactively

Think of the dynamic of calling your client as a last resort after the pet's appointment was due, and after you've have sent reminders, as opposed to calling in advance as the first step in your reminder process.

In the first scenario the client feels like a failure for not responding to your e-mail or written request to make an appointment. Your role can be perceived as being judgmental.

In the second scenario, however, your role is experienced as much more client-focused. You are calling ahead of time to ensure that the pre-arranged appointment time is convenient or to re-schedule in plenty of time to keep the annual exam on track.

Just think about how each of the above call scenarios will make your client feel and, especially, how your client will feel about your practice. We suggest calling clients four to six weeks ahead of their appointment due dates. Then, after the appointment has been confirmed or rearranged, tell the client that you will be sending a reminder.

The reminder will then be a courtesy, something expected, and a welcome piece of mail. The alternative was a source of stress that added unwelcome pressure for a client who suddenly had to juggle getting the dog to the vet between the kids soccer games on only two weeks' notice and hadn't even arranged time away from the office!

The other benefit of calling clients earlier is that it conveys the impression that your practice is extremely popular and busy. Why else would you be confirming or re-scheduling your appointments four to six weeks in advance? Who do you think is perceived as the preferred veterinary practice—the one where you can get an appointment for routine care at a moment's notice or the one that wants to confirm routine appointments six weeks in advance because they have so many other clients wanting to use that time if you can't?

SECTION 4

CLIENT REVENUE

Increase the Value of Each Client:
How to increase your profits without
increasing the number of clients you serve.

CHAPTER 18
MAXIMIZING THE AMOUNT YOUR CLIENTS SPEND IN YOUR PRACTICE

Make your product easier to buy than your competition, or you will find your customers buying from them, not you.

–Mark Cuban

Our third irrefutable Pillar of Veterinary Practice Growth is increasing the amount of revenue you generate on average from each client. Just think, if you can increase the average amount each client spends by just $10 and you have 2,000 clients then you will increase your turnover by $20,000! If the average annual value of your client is around $400, then that $10-per-client increase is the equivalent of adding fifty new clients to your practice!

Increasing the Value of Each Client

Have you ever asked yourself how many clients you need in order to have a $1,000,000 practice? The mathematics are really quite straight forward:

# of Clients	Value of Each Client	Total Value
1	$1,000,000	$1,000,000
10	$100,000	$1,000,000
100	$10,000	$1,000,000
1000	$1,000	$1,000,000
10,000	$100	$1,000,000
100,000	$10	$1,000,000
1,000,000	$1	$1,000,000

You only need one client paying $1,000,000 to have a one million dollar practice; at the other end of the scale, you need 1,000,000 clients paying you $1. Which would you rather have?

Most people would rather have the one (super) high-value client. They realize that while you'd need to do a lot for that one client, you wouldn't need to do one million times as much as for one million of the clients that only pay $1. This is a key insight.

Now we are not saying that you should have only one client. The real point is that it is more profitable (in time and money) to fully service a smaller group of clients than simply do a minimal amount of work for a larger group of clients.

Raising Prices Is Not the Only Way to Increase Client Value!

Increasing prices can be a legitimate strategy in many cases and, if you follow our coaching, we will show you how you can charge the premium prices your services deserve with little or no price resistance from clients. However, there are other ways to increase your average client value.

In our experience, the reason why many vets do not realize as much value from each client as they should is because they do not fully appreciate the privileged relationship they have with their clients. Usually a client looks up to the veterinarian (i.e., you!) as the person entrusted with the wellbeing of an important family member (i.e., their pet). You are believed to have the pet's best intentions at heart. This being the case, your recommendations will be valued and welcomed regarding any additional products or services you have to offer.

Once you fully realize the privileged position you hold as the family veterinarian, you can start to offer other products and services that you believe in and can endorse to your clients. The key here is to make sure that these recommendations and additional products and services truly do reflect the value and trust that you hold.

How to Create More Value from Each Client

Anyone who has visited a McDonald's® restaurant will have heard the phrase, "Would you like fries with that?" or the phrase that replaced it, "Would you like to make that a meal?" They will also have heard the phrase, "Would you like to Supersize that?"

These phrases are examples of strategies McDonald's uses to increase the average transaction value and ensure that each customer coming through the doors is given the opportunity to spend as much as possible.

Small Changes Can Have A Huge Impact!

In fact, McDonald's has become one of the world leaders at maximizing average transaction value. Did you know, for example, that when they introduced the question, "Would you like fries with that?" their worldwide profits doubled virtually overnight?

At this point, you may be asking what this has to do with a veterinary practice. Well, the answer is everything!

By applying some of the concepts utilized by McDonald's within your veterinary practice, you too can experience a major boost in your bottom line.

As we have discussed before there are three irrefutable ways to grow your practice:

1. Increase the number of new clients.

2. Decrease the number clients leaving.

3. Increase the amount each client spends.

These are really listed in order of difficulty and cost; i.e., the most difficult and most expensive way to grow your practice is to attract new clients, and the least difficult and least expensive way to grow your practice is to increase the amount each client spends.

Increasing the amount each client spends really depends upon two strategies:

1. **Increasing the number of times each client visits your practice.**

2. **Increasing the amount each client spends on each visit.**

What McDonald's has mastered is maximizing the amount each customer spends without increasing prices. Obviously, we are not suggesting for a second that running a veterinary practice is like operating a fast food restaurant, far from it, but the marketing principles McDonald's has developed are sound when applied to any business, including a veterinary business.

But using these same principles in your veterinary business, it is possible for you to increase your clients' average transaction value. In other words, you can increase your revenue this month with exactly the same number of client appointments as last month!

There are four principles you can use to do this, so let's take a look at each one in turn.

Up-sells

An up-sell is offering the client a more expensive version of the product or service originally requested or an add-on to the original product or service. Up-sells can be found in almost every type of business For example, here are a few examples of times when you may have been up-sold:

- Being offered luxury finishing or options on a new vehicle.
- Begin offered an extended service contract for an appliance.
- Being offered a more extensive car wash package.
- Being offered a premium brand when you didn't specify the brand you wanted (could apply to many products, e.g., tires, alcohol, gasoline, make-up, beauty products)
- Being advised to purchase more memory or a larger hard drive when having your computer serviced.
- And...being offered a super-sized meal at a fast food restaurant.

Obviously, we do not condone offering a more expensive service that is unethical or not in the animal's best interests. What we do encourage is giving your clients legitimate options and letting them decide whether they want to spend their money on them.

An up-sell should be a soft approach to helping your clients enjoy greater value from your products and services, while increasing the dollar amount of each purchase.

Some up-sells occur naturally within your practice, for example, when you check a dog's teeth during an annual check-up and find that they need cleaning. But there are other up-sells that are not so obvious.

Below are nine examples of up-sells you could be using in your practice right now:

In the exam room:

- Up-sell from an external flea prevention to a heartworm and flea prevention combined medication.
- Offer a pet owner the chance to retain their neutered pet's natural look and self-esteem with Neuticals (testicular prosthetic implants for neutered pets).
- For puppies: offer neutering.
- For senior pets: offer Glaucoma and Arthritis checks.
- For pets of all ages: Offer to microchip the pet during its annual checkup.

In the reception area:

- Offer clients a chance to save money by buying bigger bags of dog food or bigger bottles of shampoo.
- Offer three bags of food for the price of two or offer a second bag at half-price.

- Offer a more expensive or brand name lead, collar, harness, etc.

- Have a bowl of dog chews at $1 each to reward dogs for good behavior during the visit.

Down-sells

Just as important as up-sells, but very underutilized, are down-sells. A down-sell is when you offer your client something less expensive when they have turned down the chance to purchase a more expensive item.

For example, let's say you have just explained to a client the reasons and benefits for heartworm medication. You have presented a well known heartworm treatment that should be given monthly but will cost $120 for a twelve month supply.

If your presentation was good enough, then the price will not be a problem if it is within budget. But if the client truly cannot afford to pull out $120 in addition to the day's other fees, then you need a down-sell. In this case you could offer a six-month supply for $69. (In parts of the country where heartworm is not a year round problem, this may be the first offer.)

If that is still outside the comfort zone, you could then offer a single monthly dose for $14. The smaller expense of $14 is manageable, the client appreciates your giving them that option, and leaving the clinic with some heartworm medication.

Anything that legitimately and ethically gives your clients a reason to visit your practice every month should be seen as a good thing, as it gives you the opportunity to offer something else at every visit, such as food, shampoo, etc.

Another example of a down-sell would be where you have

recommended some shampoo to a client. There are two different down-sell options here.

First, you stock two different brands of shampoo and you offer the most expensive one first. The client will either happily pay or ask for something less expensive. Your down-sell is to offer them the less expensive one.

Alternatively, it is usual that the best value bottle for the client is the larger size so you offer them that one first. Again they will either pay or quibble with the price. If they quibble, you can explain the value benefits of the larger bottle and then down-sell them to a smaller size if price is still an issue.

The key point about up-sells and down-sells is that you are giving your clients options at different price points. Some clients want to ensure that their pets get the best you have to offer and they expect to pay a premium to get it, whereas others will be pleased that you are able to offer them a less expensive alternative to something they want but can't afford.

Cross-sells

A cross-sell is where you offer your client the chance to purchase another product or service in addition to the original service or product they purchased. "Would you like fries with that?" is a classic example of a cross-sell.

Other common cross-sells are:

- On Amazon.com™ after you have selected a product, they will show you a list of related products.
- At the hairdresser, a stylist will often offer to sell a take-home supply of the products that were just used for the client's hair.

- In the shoe department, you may be offered weather-protecting spray or polish for the shoes you purchase.

Here a few examples of cross-sells you can use in your veterinary business:

- Offer diet food for dogs with weight issues.
- Offer non-stripping shampoo for dogs taking external flea treatment.
- Offer grooming at a promotional price if it is booked and paid for during a veterinary appointment.
- Ask if the client needs pet toys, leads, collars, bowls, or other accessories.
- Have an Offer-of-the-Week or Offer-of-the-Month on display in the reception area.
- Offer training classes for puppies and behavioral classes for adult dogs during the visit.
- Create a catalogue of the products you stock or can get. Have copies of the catalog available in your reception area for waiting clients to read and/or take home.
- Offer other pet-related services such as pet-sitting, dog-walking, day care, and boarding. If you can't or won't offer them yourself, then partner with a company that does and collect a commission for each client you refer.

Bundles

Bundles is the term used for bundling together related products and selling the bundle for less than the combined prices of the individual items sold separately.

Bundles are an excellent way to boost sales and increase client satisfaction. Recommending bundles will endear you to clients (you're helping them save money), hence increasing client satisfaction.

The most common example of a bundle is the meal option at a fast food restaurant. However, even expensive restaurants use this ploy with set menus or banquet menus. Your local sports retailer sells bundles, such as a soccer bundle containing shoes, ball, and guards for a special price, or a tennis bundle containing racket, balls, and tennis shirts.

The most obvious bundle to offer in your veterinary practice is a puppy starter kit that contains bowls, food, bedding, toys, and similar baby items. You could have different levels of bundle from just the few products listed above to a complete service-and-product package that might include a voucher for neutering when the time is right, micro-chipping, worming tablets, flea medication, vaccinations, and more.

Other bundles you could offer include:

- Shampoo, bathmats, and towels.
- Food, bowl, food scoop, and food mat.
- Collar, leads, car harness, and identity tag.
- Dental checkup, dental chews, and finger brushes.

Make a list of every major product line you stock, then think of the related items you could bundle with it. You don't have to use them all but it will give you plenty of options for the future and also help you think about the placement of your products in your practice reception. Remember, you are helping your practice by helping the client to get everything they need at a great value.

Avoid These Mistakes

Applying up-sells, down-sells, cross-sells, and bundles within your practice is a great way to increase the average client transaction value and boost your profits significantly. There are some common mistakes that you must avoid, however, if these techniques are to be successful.

1. Not Doing It!

The biggest mistake you can make, of course, is not implementing these strategies in the first place. If you are not currently using at least one up-sell, down-sell, cross-sell or bundle, you're leaving thousands of dollars on the table every year!

2. Being Too Pushy

The second biggest mistake is being too pushy with your client. Anyone who has bought an electrical appliance or computer will have encountered the too-pushy salesperson trying to sell an extended warranty. That is as far as you can get from what you need to do in your practice.

If you've already established rapport, identified needs, summarized, presented benefits, and handled objections, then up/down/cross-selling is just presenting an opportunity in a casual manner. If the client says "No," don't push it and don't cause discomfort. Remember, you're playing a percentage game, and you can't win them all!

3. Having An Unconvincing Manner

If you or your staff don't believe that what you are offering to sell is of benefit to the client, then don't expect the client to believe it either! Make sure that your purchasing opportunities are to the client's benefit, and then offer them with confidence.

Effective Strategies

Being positive is the key. You've got to assume that naturally the client will want what you're offering. Begin the up-sell with a brief benefit statement, then if possible, say what's unique about your product. To avoid sounding pushy, particularly if the up-sell requires some elaboration, ask for the client's permission to describe it.

Create scripts for your staff to practice, and don't try to introduce too many sales at once. Start small and introduce more as you and your staff gain confidence. For example, you could start with a script for your front desk staff. "Rover's been such a good boy today, would you like to reward him with a tasty chew? I can't just add it to your bill if you like."

Other Ways to Increase Average Transaction Value

Up-sells, cross-sells, down-sells and bundles are strategies that you can use every day in your practice. They are fundamentally ways to increase the value of each client during conversations you and your team have every day with your clients.

There are, however, some other strategic ways you increase your average client value.

Internal Marketing

We've already shown you how you can attract new clients to your practice but the biggest untapped source of revenue at your disposal is the list of clients you have in your veterinary management system, your currently active clients and your previous clients who have become inactive. That list of pet owners with their addresses is a veritable gold mine just waiting to be excavated!

In the section on Client Retention we showed you how you could include offers each month to persuade clients to come into your practice. Well, these offers can also be sent in other ways. A key part of your strategy to increase your average client revenue should be to tempt your active and inactive clients with time sensitive offers. For example, February is traditionally Dental Month but there is no reason why August (six months later) couldn't be Dental Month too.

Now, if you can find five other offers that you can run six months apart, you will have a campaign to run every month. Here are some other campaigns that will entice your clients into your practice in between annual visits:

- Arthritis—Orthopedic Exams
- Senior Dog
- Pet Insurance
- Weight Loss
- Skin Complaints
- Fleas and Heartworm
- Offers on products (food, toys etc)

Once you have decided on your offers there are many options at your disposal for getting them into the hands of your clients. All of the direct mail options we showed you in the Client Attraction section are applicable to send to your active and inactive client lists although, the message to each of these lists may want to be slightly different.

You should have the e-mail addresses of your clients (make this part of your client joining process if it isn't already) so you can email them with offers or as part of your multi-step process. Remember, the worst number in marketing is one!

You can also put offers on your Facebook page each month where many of your clients may be able to see them.

Raise Your Fees

While we acknowledge that there are other ways to increase customer value besides price, that does not mean that you should be underselling your services. You cannot build a successful practice by being the least expensive; you run the risk that someone will come along who offers even lower prices.

Most pet owners do not choose their veterinarians based solely on price, so you need to focus on delivering the service, care, and experience that takes price out of the equation. Even in this economy, only 15% of your clients are likely to make their choices based on price. Of course, as we have already said, if your service is perceived as a commodity, **all** purchasers will shop for the cheapest price.

The majority of your clients will choose you because they have been referred by another client, they believe you deliver good value, you have a reputation for high quality, or your location is convenient.

Do not fall into the trap of equating value for money with being cheap. For example, Apple iPad users will tell you that they have got great value for the very substantial amount of money they have spent, as will Porsche drivers, and Lakers fans who paid thousands for courtside seats to see Kobe deliver yet another NBA Championship.

Even small increases in price can have a significant impact on your bottom line, so make sure you are charging fees that match the quality of your service, care, and client experience. Remember, the saying that "you get what you pay for" is still alive and well, and charging too little can actually cause you to lose business among the affluent who expect to pay top prices for top-level service.

Introduce a Deluxe Version of Your Services

One thing you can do immediately to increase your profits is to offer a deluxe version of one or more of your services. You will find that when given the choice between the basic version and the deluxe or premium version, at least 20% of your clients will choose the deluxe version, provided that you have added enough value to the deluxe version.

The caveat here is that there should be no difference in the quality of the actual patient care; first-rate veterinary medicine is provided to pets receiving both the basic and the deluxe version of a service. The difference will be in the overall client experience. For example, a deluxe version could offer appointment times at shorter notice or at special times during the day, transportation of the pet, guaranteed minimum waiting times, or even extra screenings for certain predispositions.

From spas to car washes, there are always different levels of service available at different price points. It is human nature that a certain percentage of the population will always go for the best option available, if only for the prestige associated with it. Veterinary care is no different.

CHAPTER 19
THE POWER OF CONTINUITY INCOME

Whenever you see a successful business, someone once made a courageous decision

–Peter Drucker

Every veterinary practice and, in our view, every company should have some form of continuity income.

Continuity income results from your client's payment of a monthly fee in return for a product or service. The fee is usually charged to the credit card or bank account at the beginning of each month.

Continuity programs have been around for years in various forms. Health Club membership is a classic example of a continuity program, as are Book-of-the-Month Clubs.

Before you make the assumption that you couldn't implement a continuity program within your veterinary practice, let's look at a couple of examples of well run and well received continuity programs currently being offered by some unlikely businesses.

Continuity Program Examples

Diane Coutu runs a take-out pizza restaurant in Winnipeg, Ontario, Canada. Despite competing with 2-for-1, 3-for-1 and even 4-for-the-price-of-1 pizza take-out restaurants, Diane's Gourmet Pizzeria is able to charge as much as $32 for pizza in a city not noted for being the most upscale part of the world. It has more in common with Youngstown, Ohio, than Malibu, California!

While there is little doubt that what Diane is selling is a commodity, it's clear that she's been able change the perception of the commodity by positioning herself in the market as a gourmet pizza take-out and by creating status through membership levels in her restaurant's continuity program.

You see, Diane has dozens of members who pay her at the start of each month to receive *Diane Dollars*, which they can use to buy pizza at her restaurant. The program works by giving members extras for the money they spend. For example, her Silver level costs $25 per month and members receive $30 worth of Diane Dollars plus bonuses; Gold members pay $50 and receive $65 worth of Diane Dollars plus bonuses and extra gifts.

The program works so well that Diane has doubled her business since introducing it! She has found that members not only tend to spend more than their membership fees each month but more than all her other customers put together.

Our second example of a continuity program in an unlikely business is Kennedy's All-American Barber Club. Kennedy's is a fast growing franchise trying to recreate "a time when men were men," when getting a straight-razor shave and a haircut was the civilized thing to do.

While you can make an appointment or just walk in to have a haircut or straight-razor shave, what makes Kennedy's different is its membership continuity program. Kennedy's has four levels of membership.

The Basic Gentleman® costs $40 per month and includes unlimited haircuts, complimentary beverage during each visit, and complimentary Kennedy's Lifestyle Magazine.

The top of the line is membership in Life®, starting at $120 per month. For this, members are entitled to "Unlimited Signature Haircuts, Unlimited Signature Haircuts for your children under 13, Unlimited Straight Razor Shaves, Unlimited Mini-Facials and Waxing, Priority Reservations, Private Humidor-Style Mini-Locker customized with nameplate crafted just for you, 20% Discount on all Kennedy's™ Grooming Products, complimentary beverage during each visit, Black & White framed 8×10 Photo with your business card inserted and hung on the Wall-of-Fame, yearly Birthday Present from your local Kennedy's™ Proprietor, Concierge/Personal Shopper Services, Complimentary Kennedy's™ Lifestyle Magazine, Nationwide Usage Rights at all other Kennedy's™ (with a minor courtesy charge), shoeshine during service."

Now the thought of having over $120 deducted from their bank accounts each month by the local barber shop may make some men want to grow their hair long, but those are not the men Kennedy's wants to attract. The Kennedy's target market is affluent men, just as we have suggested you should try to attract affluent pet owners.

As you can see from the list of items that make up their top membership level, the haircut (which is a commodity to most men) becomes incidental within the package of the whole experience. This is a great example of how selling an experience and repackaging what you offer can significantly increase the value of your product or service.

Lessons Learned

There are three great lessons to learn from Diane's Gourmet Pizzeria and Kennedy's All-American Barber Club:

1. The affluent are alive and well and spending money.

2. Being different is key to positioning your business within your marketplace.

3. If a pizza store and a barber shop can run successful continuity programs for affluent clients, then it should be possible to do the same within a veterinary practice!

The Benefits of Continuity

You can readily infer the many advantages of implementing a continuity program within your veterinary practice. Let's itemize those benefits and examine each more closely.

Improved Cash Flow

One of the main benefits of continuity income is that it is regular. At the start of each month, before you have even opened your doors and switched the lights on, you have money in the bank. This does wonders for your cash flow.

For example, if you had 300 clients paying $50 per month to be in your continuity program you would start each month with $15,000 in your practice bank account! This helps stabilize your revenue and allow you more accurately to forecast your income.

It is important to note here that although monthly continuity is preferable, quarterly fees have also worked very well and may be more suitable depending on the nature of your clientele and your continuity program.

Increased Client Value

Generally clients within continuity programs will be worth more to your practice than your other clients, because their annual expenditures will be more than if they were not in the program.

This is to the clients' advantage because, while they can afford the monthly payments, they may not be able to afford to pay all at once for everything they get as part of the program.

Remember, individuals have cash flow challenges too, so the opportunity to pay for something on a monthly basis is often welcome. How many people would never take out health club memberships if they had to pay for the entire year in advance?

Down here in Orlando, even the theme parks are introducing continuity, with the option to pay monthly for theme park passes. This allows them to tap into a whole new community of customers who may not have been able to afford or justify pulling out several hundred dollars for tickets but who can afford the smaller monthly payments.

Increased Frequency of Spending

Regardless of the type of continuity program you implement, the very nature of a continuity program means that members will visit your practice more often. Each time they visit should be an opportunity for them to spend money in your practice, even if it is only to purchase dog food, chews, or other incidental items.

There is also the possibility that, if any of the additional visits require a pet to be seen by a veterinarian, then other conditions may be discovered. This doesn't just increase your client's expenditure, it's good medicine. You will undoubtedly detect some ailments earlier than if the client were visiting just once a year.

Increased Emotional Commitment

When your clients are committed to paying you monthly for service, they will have a much bigger emotional connection to your practice than if they were non-members. This emotional commitment means they are unlikely to go elsewhere.

As a side note, we should mention that membership cards will make your clients feel more connected to your continuity programs and thus to your practice.

More Referrals

Continuity programs work because they provide something your clients value and want. And continuity members are more committed to your practice. When you combine these two factors, you get members who will be great advocates of your program.

When you also consider that any continuity program you initiate in your practice is unlikely to be available in other practices near you, your program can become a real talking point among members and their pet-owning friends. As long as you are delivering a consistently good experience, your continuity members will be only too eager to refer others to become members of the same club.

Levels of Membership

As you saw with the pizza and barber shop examples, membership levels work extremely well within continuity programs. One reason for this is that some people like the status and aspirational identification that comes with being in the higher-priced level.

It also allows you to put an ascension model in place, allowing members paying at the lower level to be upgraded to a higher level as part of an up-sell, as a reward for length of membership, or as a symbol (to themselves and others) of mobility and achievement.

It also allows you to cater to the different levels of income among your clientele by providing different membership levels at different price points.

Micro-continuity

Generally, continuity programs have no end dates, only anniversary or renewal dates. However, there may be cases when you wish to provide a membership program that only lasts a certain length of time, depending the nature of the service being offered.

These closed-end programs are called micro-continuity programs because they relatively brief, generally lasting only a few weeks or months before expiring at a predefined end date.

Can Continuity Work in Your Veterinary Practice?

Now that you've seen what continuity is, the benefits these programs bring to your practice, and some of their mechanics of operation, can you imagine a continuity program within your own veterinary practice?

Take five or ten minutes to list the places in your practice where such a program could work. Note: that's **could** work, not couldn't work. The key to exploring anything new in your practice is to think first of the ways it **could** work.

The answer to whether continuity can work in your practice is absolutely yes, but only if you are open to the idea and understand that continuity is something that can be of great benefit to your clients as well as to you.

Remember, continuity programs are a good thing for you and your clients if you design them to benefit your clients and their pets.

Continuity Opportunities for Veterinary Practices

If you haven't realized it already, think about the obvious continuity income opportunities that many veterinary practices are already implementing, such as monthly flea treatments (e.g., Sentinel), although these tend to be annual or semi-annual payments.

In order to think of the not-so-obvious opportunities, examine the areas of your practice where you could provide great value for something your clients need for their pets that could being funded on a monthly or quarterly basis.

Here are four ideas:

Preventative Dentistry

We hear of many clients bringing their pets for a dental checkup, especially during Pet Dental Month in February, and then refusing the recommended cleaning because of the price tag. An ongoing preventative dentistry program is a good way to avoid this sticker shock and provide better for appropriate medical care.

Could you offer your clients quarterly dental checkups and an annual dental cleaning (if necessary) for a fixed monthly fee? Your program might include bonuses, such as a monthly supply of dental chews or a complimentary home cleaning kit.

Because dental checkups are fairly quick and can be

performed by a veterinary nurse, you should be able to work out a very competitive and compelling monthly fee.

Note: If you're worried about people defaulting, e.g. stopping the monthly payments as soon as their pet has had the big expense (the cleaning), don't be. The majority of your clients will be honest.

Besides, there are means of minimizing the impact of a defaulting client, perhaps by asking for an initial deposit (initiation fee) two or three times the monthly payment amount. This works well for orthodontists who collect a substantial deposit at the outset when they do most of the work on kids' braces, then prorate the remaining fees over the number of months expected to be required for completing treatment.

Disney has adopted similar measures here in Orlando. Guests pay an enrollment deposit equivalent to the price of one day's admission when they join the new monthly payment program for annual theme park passes.

Weight Loss/Weight Control Program

Pet obesity is an increasing problem and another one that lends itself to continuity care. Could you put a program in place that provides a pet diet and exercise program with weekly, bi-weekly, or monthly weigh-ins? The program fee could include food, or members could buy food at a reduced rate.

Annual Wellness Program

On a broader scale, perhaps you could give your clients the opportunity to pay for next year's checkup throughout the year by enrolling their pets in an annual wellness program. This program could also let them purchase pet food, chews, toys, grooming, boarding, and even other veterinary services at a reduced rate.

This type of program has minimum risk to you because the client effectively starts paying for the appointment twelve months ahead of time, contributing each month until the appointment arrives. At that point, the only thing the client should have to pay for would be any extras required in addition to the standard examination.

If the patient presents because of a health issue at any time before the annual appointment, then members could pay for the treatment separately, perhaps at a reduced rate for being in the program, or you could reduce the fee by the amount already paid into the program.

Client Privilege or Loyalty Card

Taking a leaf from Diane Coutu's book, you could have your own membership card that clients pay for monthly in return for Doggy Dollars or Kitty Kash to spend in your practice. For example, $25 per month could earn $30 in reward "cash" to spend in your practice on anything they like.

If they are committed to paying you $30 or $50 per month, will they go elsewhere for pet care or supplies? Not very likely!

There are many other opportunities within your practice to introduce continuity programs to benefit both you and your clients. Remember, you must be different from your competitors to stand out from the crowd in the New Economy. Continuity programs are certainly one way to achieve that.

All you need is the courage and the conviction to embrace them and the creativity to design them!

SECTION 5

LAYING THE FOUNDATIONS FOR SUCCESS

Creating an environment for everyday success in your veterinary practice.

CHAPTER 20
SYSTEMS: THE PATH TO BUSINESS SUCCESS

Organize around business functions, not people.
Build systems within each business function.
Let systems run the business and people run the systems.
People come and go but the systems remain constant.

–Michael Gerber (*E-Myth Revisited*)

Most veterinary practice owners have one or more of the following aspirations for their future:

1. Have more vacation time.

2. Build a chain of veterinary practices, even if that means just owning two practices instead of one.

3. Retire but keep the practice and enjoy the continuing profits.

4. Sell the practice for a nice profit to support retirement.

The good news we have for you is that all these aspirations

are attainable. The caveat is this: if you want to attain the first three goals without increasing your stress levels or the fourth without reducing your windfall, you must systematize your practice.

If you have already read the best-selling book *The E-Myth Revisited* by Michael Gerber, then you are already sold on the subject of systems. If you haven't read it, then we recommend that you get yourself a copy and read it now. Gerber's theory is that most businesses fail because they are not founded by entrepreneurs, who work on the business, but by technicians, who work in the business.

His premise as we apply it to the veterinary profession is that veterinarians are technicians who work in the veterinary business. Vets make the fatal assumption that just because they understand how to do the technical work of their business—i.e., they know how to practice veterinary medicine—they also understand how to build a practice to deliver that work.

The reasoning behind this argument is that as veterinarians start their own practices, they build practices that are heavily dependent on their own skills, talents, interests, and tendencies. The veterinarian therefore ends up devoting his time, energy, and life to working for a living, even if he is self-employed, until finally he sells his job for break-even or even a net loss on all of the investment of his career.

Does this ring any uncomfortable bells for you?

The entrepreneurial veterinarian, on the other hand, builds a practice that can run itself in the hands of professional management, giving her the time to invest in other businesses or whatever else she wants to do with her life. The practice provides an income that she does not have to work for and provides a valuable asset for her future. In effect the entrepreneurial veterinarian builds an enterprise that can be grown as big as she wants it to be.

Isn't that the sort of practice that you dreamed of building?

To quote Michael Gerber:

"...your practice must be designed so that it can do what it does systematically, predictably, every single time."

By introducing systems, you can create a consistent excellent experience for every single client every single time.

Why is McDonald's the most successful franchise of all time and the most successful burger restaurant? Well, it sure isn't the quality of their food; it's easy to find better quality burgers. The answer is their systems. Once they have determined the most efficient and cost-effective way to do something, everybody does it that way every time and everywhere, and customers keep coming because they know what to expect. A McDonald's in Seattle uses exactly the same operations manual as a McDonald's in Orlando or New York or London or Sydney.

McDonald's rings up the profits because it is a systems-dependent business, not a people-dependent business. You must develop a systems-dependent practice, rather than a people-dependent practice. Please don't think that we are for one second equating what you do with what McDonald's does. We are just using them as an example of the ultimate systematized business.

When you build systems into your practice, you create a number of very tangible benefits:

- Your customers will be happier knowing that they will get a consistently high-quality experience every time they visit your practice. They will also learn that they get the same experience no matter which veterinarian they see, which makes them more flexible about which doctor attends their pets.

- Your staff will be happier with a predictable way of doing things. People who are not natural leaders need instructions, and systems give them that. People who are subject to evaluation want to know what procedures they are expected to follow and what standards they are expected to meet; systems give them that too.

- You will be happier knowing that every consultation will be done the way you want it to be.

- You will be less reliant on any single individual once new support staff can be trained efficiently to follow the systems that have been created for performance of their duties. Prospective and new veterinarians will know how things are done in your practice and what your way is. (Staff members who have held you to ransom over your suspicion that the practice can't run without them no longer have this power.)

- You will be able to take time off from your practice, safe in the knowledge that things are being done as you have prescribed while you're away, and that your practice will still be in one piece when you get back.

- If you want to open another practice you will already have the blueprint and systems manuals required to get it up and running very quickly with a high degree of certainty that it will be successful.

- If you already have more than one practice, you can be sure that things will be so consistent across practices that staff from one practice can cover for staff at another without missing a step.

- Your practice is much more attractive to potential buyers, who prefer to purchase a turnkey operation that runs itself.

So what kinds of systems do you need to introduce?

To answer this question, start thinking about the key processes in your practice, consider how they should work to be optimally effective, and then begin to design procedures with written instructions that will ensure they are done this way each and every time.

A good starting point is to think of the different departments within your practice, e.g., Reception, Consulting Rooms, Back Office, Boarding, and any others you designate. Each department should have its own systems. Here are some examples:

Reception Area Systems

Every client should receive a consistent first-class experience, and every member of staff working in the reception area must know exactly what to do to assure it. Here is a sample of some of the systems you should have in place to enable your reception staff to do their jobs properly:

- Answering the telephone.
- Greeting clients.
- Pre-consultation.
- Post-consultation.
- Dealing with complaints.

- Dealing with accidents.

Consulting Room Systems

Systems for your veterinarians and veterinary technicians to follow in the consulting room are even more important in ensuring first-class patient care and a consistent, high-quality experience for your clients. The idea is not to constrain their abilities as veterinary practitioners but to ensure that mistakes do not occur and that consultations and procedures are carried out in the way you want them to be conducted.

Examples of consulting room systems include:

- New patient protocols.
- Your systems for diagnosis.
- Your systems for treatment

Marketing Systems

Your back office obviously should have systems for patient record keeping, accounting, and dealing with staff issues, but we are going to focus on our specialty, the systems that most veterinary practices don't even think about—Marketing Systems.

Marketing systems are generally created in the back office and then deployed throughout the practice. At the very least you should have systems in place for client referral, testimonial collection, selling, client reactivation, and direct response. We'll look at each of these systems separately.

Client Referral System

A good referral system will save you thousands of dollars in marketing and create a steady flow of new clients to your practice. One of the keys to referral success is a system to make it run smoothly. Your staff needs procedures for encouraging referral, rewarding clients who refer, tracking who has referred whom, and greeting newly referred clients entering your practice.

Testimonial Collection System

Since the next best thing after a referral is a testimonial, you must have a system in place to collect testimonials for your marketing and your Website that will have such credibility that your competitors won't know what hit them. Part of your process should be procedures to get video testimonials from happy clients before they leave they practice or, at very least, ask them to write comments in a testimonial book.

Up-sell/Cross-sell/Down-sell Systems

You need to have systems in place to ensure that clients visiting your practice are offered the opportunity to purchase other things that they need. Your procedures and standards should specify what extras your team should be offering that are congruent with a client's visit and also provide scripts for each one, so that the message is not diluted or otherwise miscommunicated.

Client Reactivation System

Ideally, you have already put client retention systems in place by improving your approach to appointment scheduling. But you must also have a system that alerts you when clients inevitably slip through the net and don't meet their annual appointments. When clients become inactive, you must have a system in place to attempt to reactivate and get them back on board.

Too many veterinary practices give up on clients who, with a little bit of encouragement and feeling that they haven't been forgotten about, would happily come back. You should be able to track inactive clients and monitor the steps your practice has taken to get each one back.

Direct Response Marketing Systems

Earlier we introduced you to Direct Response Marketing and the Direct Response Marketing Funnel. In order to maximize these powerful strategies, you need to put systems in place to manage them.

There should be systems for marketing to prospects, systems for making offers to existing clients, and systems for generating new leads. Each system should include detailed procedures for all the steps required; for example, placing ads, tracking responses, and fulfilling offers.

There should be procedures specifying how to follow up with the prospects who respond to your initial offers and how to convert prospects to paying clients.

Over time, you will be able to predict how many new prospects and clients a campaign is likely to attract and know with great certainty how much you will need to invest to generate a lead and attract a client.

CHAPTER 21
FAIL TO PLAN, PLAN TO FAIL!

Think ahead. Don't let day-to-day operations drive out planning.

–Donald Rumsfeld

For too many veterinary practices, marketing is a crisis reaction to a decline in new clients or a drop in income rather than a proactively planned year round activity. The most successful veterinary practices, however, plan their marketing activities twelve months in advance.

Continual marketing means that you are constantly adding new clients and, just as importantly, through internal marketing you are increasing the amount your clients spend and constantly preventing your current clients from being lured away by other practices. As marketing becomes a part of your everyday practice life and the lifeblood of your practice, you gain a huge advantage over practices that don't plan their marketing.

By planning your marketing in advance, so that you have a consistent strategy every month for generating more revenue, you keep yourself off the rollercoaster of income increases following a promotion one month followed by revenue drops when the promotion ends the following month.

The easiest way to manage this is to create a marketing calendar for your practice. This will let everyone in the practice know what your marketing focus is going to be each month and which marketing pieces are going to be mailed. Each month should have a page showing key marketing tasks for the month and who is responsible for them, along with key dates, such as newsletter deliveries and promotion end dates.

Figure 11 shows such a sample marketing calendar. Note that there are targets for the month at the top of the page, as well as landmarks such as number of calendar days in the month and number of days the practice is open. We suggest that you also use a 12-month wall planner that shows key marketing activities and events for the entire calendar year.

You may find it easier to plan if you choose a theme for each month. Your themes might be based on the offers you have scheduled—for example, Dental Month—or you might organize them around significant holidays and events of the month—such as Thanksgiving or Independence Day.

Plan to do both internal marketing (to your current clients) and external marketing (to prospective clients) throughout the year. Also, remember that a twelve-month marketing plan doesn't require twelve different offers. Six campaigns repeated twice a year is perfectly acceptable.

Make sure you get your team involved in planning your year's marketing activities. You may be surprised at what they come up with! This is a great opportunity to create a buzz of excitement within your practice. There's no doubt that when everyone knows what's going on and what's coming up, your marketing will be far more successful.

If you think this sounds like a lot of work, you're right. It is a lot of work, but the rewards are worth it. Make no mistake: marketing your practice is as important to your success as any other function of your veterinary business. Be sure to treat it with respect.

Marketing Activities for January 2011

Calendar Days This Month: 31 **Practice Open Days This Month:** 25

This Months Targets	New Clients: 30	Reactivated Clients: 5
	New Client Referrals: 10	Testimonials: 25

Holidays	**Special Events This Month**
Saturday 1st - New Years Day	
Monday 17th - Martin Luther King Jr. Day	
Friday 14th - Dress Up Your Pet Day	

Internal Marketing Tasks

Task	Person	Deadline
Prepare Client Reactivation Letters	Lisa	1/6
Mail Out Client Reactivation Letters	Debbie	1/7
Prepare February Newsletter Content	Lisa	1/14
Finalize Newsletter Offers	Dr. Jones	1/14
Get Newsletter to Printers	Lisa	1/17
Mail Out Newsletter to Clients	Debbie	1/27
Track January Referrals	Lisa	1/31
Mail Out December Referral Rewards	Debbie	1/5
Collate Testimonials— Videos/Photos/Letters	Lisa	Fridays
Implement Testimonials—Website/Reception TV/Newsletter	Lisa	Mondays
Prepare Dental Month Offer Letters	Lisa	1/21
Mail Out Dental Month Letters	Debbie	1/28

External Marketing Tasks

Task	Person	Deadline
Design Dental Ad for Newspaper	Lisa	1/21
Place Dental Ad in Newspaper	Debbie	1/31
Update Website with Dental Offer	Lisa	1/31

Figure 11 - Marketing Calendar Example

One of the reasons we suggest creating a marketing calendar for your veterinary practice is because marketing is a full time, year round activity. If you are serious about doing it right, then you will not only take an active interest in it yourself, you will get your team involved and make sure that someone in your practice is responsible for making it happen.

If you own a large practice, you may want to consider employing someone full time as your "marketing department." If your practice is fairly small, however, then you can probably share the tasks between a couple of your existing team members.

Whatever you do, do not leave your marketing to chance. Make it a planned activity that is an everyday part of life in your practice. This will put you ahead of 95% of veterinary practices, so embrace it now before your competitors do!

CHAPTER 22
MASTERMIND GROUPS: YOUR SUPPORT NETWORK FOR SUCCESS

Analyze the record of any person who has accumulated great fortune, and many of those who have accumulated modest fortunes, and you will find that they have either consciously, or unconsciously employed the Master Mind principle.

–Napoleon Hill

Let's face it, the road to business success can be a lonely one. Even when you have achieved whatever you define as success, you may still feel like an oddball among your friends and family.

You see, not everyone has the same entrepreneurial inclinations that you have. Many of your friends and family accept that the "normal" thing to do is work for a company eight hours a day, five days a week. The fact that you work for yourself and work longer hours is often perceived as strange. Despite any success you have had, many are only too willing to criticize your ideas and tell you where you are going wrong!

Most veterinary practice owners have only three choices when they come up with a new idea for their practice:

1. Share it with a friend or family member.

2. Share it with their staff.

3. Implement it without discussing it with anyone.

The problem with sharing it with friends and family is that, unless they are successful in business themselves, they are not well qualified to give you feedback and advice, even though they may be very willing to offer it! The problem with sharing your ideas with your staff is that their feedback is likely to be based on how it will affect them, or what they think you want to hear, and not based on the greater good of the practice. Of course, the problem of not sharing your ideas with anyone is that you are can make some painful and costly mistakes that could have been avoided by objective evaluation.

A better idea is to seek out the help of other successful business people.

In 1937, in his classic book *Think and Grow Rich*, Napoleon Hill introduced his thirteen principles of success, based on his study of over five hundred of the most successful and wealthy persons on the planet. These individuals included some of the most brilliant minds of the time such as Henry Ford, William Wrigley, Jr., Charles M. Schwab, John D. Rockefeller, Thomas Edison, and Dr Alexander Graham Bell.

Arguably the most important principle Hill introduced was that of the Master Mind. In fact, one of Hill's stories tells how

Henry Ford's business really began to accelerate when he started to form alliances with some of the other great and successful businessmen of his generation.

So what is a Mastermind Group? Hill's definition is "coordination of knowledge and effort, in a spirit of harmony, between two or more people, for the attainment of a definite purpose."

The type of mastermind group Hill described in *Think & Grow Rich* was a group of people with various skills gathered together by one person to focus on the success and vision of that one person. In small business terms, this is the equivalent of recruiting a group of successful peers to act as an advisory panel to your practice. The idea is that each member of the group brings some special knowledge that will help guide you and your practice toward reaching your goals.

Because this type of mastermind group relies on others giving up their time solely for the benefit of one person, the meetings would generally be one-on-one between the organizer and the advisors, and more likely than not in the form of telephone conversations or e-mails rather than face-to-face or group meetings.

A much more common form of mastermind group, and the one we prefer, is the one in which a group of like-minded persons meet with the focus of helping all the persons in the group to achieve their goals. Traditionally, these meetings are held in person around a table, but with today's technology, they could take place via teleconferencing or even over the Internet.

In case you're a little wary of what you might be letting yourself in for if you were to join a mastermind group, here's an overview of what you can expect.

A good mastermind group will be led by a facilitator who

will lay down the ground rules and make sure that time is allocated equally and fairly. Usually each member of the group will have a chance to tell the other members what has happened since the last meeting and to ask the group for help and advice on goal achievement. The other members of the group will then do their best to offer ideas, advice, support, and encouragement.

Each member usually gets around thirty minutes of total focus on his or her business. While this does not sound like a lot, there are two things that make it valuable. First, at the end of that half hour, you are very likely to have more ideas than you can handle in one month and at least one action point to implement before the next meeting. Second, you will also get to hear and participate in the discussions of the other members' businesses, generating even more insights and ideas for your own business.

At some of the better meetings, the facilitator will bring in an expert on some business growth topic to make a short presentation to the group. This gives you ideas for your business and also sparks discussion among the group, leading to even more ideas. With all-day meetings, lunch is usually provided so that the meeting can resume without the delay caused by waiting for members to return from outside.

Be assured that a mastermind group provides a very non-judgmental environment where all ideas and information shared are heard respectfully and kept confidential. You will enjoy getting out of your practice and into a place where you can get a fresh perspective on your business.

In a moment we'll take a look at the two types of mastermind group that we believe success-seeking veterinary practice owners should join. First, let's summarize the benefits of joining a mastermind group.

The Benefits Of Joining A Mastermind Group

1. Sounding Board for Ideas

A mastermind group is a great place to get feedback on new ideas. You will get to hear different opinions about why your idea may or may not work, and there is a good chance that one of the other members may have already tried it. This second-hand knowledge can save you a fortune if it helps you avoid foreseeable mistakes or relinquish ideas that have no chance of return on investment.

As you get to know and trust the members in your mastermind group, you will feel confident about the advice they give. This can prove invaluable when testing new ideas.

2. Source of New Ideas

Whether you're discussing your own issues or those of another member, you will be sure to pick up a wealth of new ideas. The key is to listen to what is working for other businesses and then ask yourself how the same thing could work in your veterinary business. You will also benefit from every member of the group freely giving you their ideas about how to resolve the issues and challenges you face in your business. Of course, not every idea you hear will be right for you, but some will be; you choose for yourself which ones to take away with you.

3. Mutual Support

Whatever is happening in your business, good or bad, you can be sure of the support of a group of fellow business owners who understand what you're going through and have probably gone through the same thing themselves. If you have success, they will be there to cheer you; if you have had a failure, they will be there to pick you up and help you get back on track.

4. Motivation

One of the great things about mastermind groups is that you almost always leave with so many ideas and action plans that you will be eager to get back to your practice and start to implement them. Combine this with the encouragement you receive from the group, and you will have all the motivation you need to increasing the success of your practice.

5. Accountability

A key part of any successful mastermind group is that, after each meeting, each member comes away with actions with deadlines that they commit to taking to improve their business. This is very powerful, because at the next meeting the other members in your mastermind group will hold you accountable for following through on the actions you committed to taking. As a business owner, you would not normally be accountable to anyone; you are entirely free to procrastinate. This friendly accountability from your mastermind group will help you get things done!

6. Differing Perspectives

Every member of the mastermind group gets to help you with your business challenges and you get to help with theirs. This means that when you present an idea or problem to the group, you hear a variety of perspectives on it that may make you think differently about it or approach it in a different way.

The members of your group may also be able to see your business as a whole in a totally different light and suggest other income streams and new ways to attract clients. Of course, just taking time away from your practice to work on your practice can give you a completely different perspective on the areas where you need to focus.

7. Synergy

Synergy is defined as:

"The interaction of two or more agents or forces so that their combined effect is greater than the sum of their individual effects."

This characterizes mastermind groups, and when several people come together with the aim of improving your business, the results can be astonishing. One brain focused on your business is a powerful thing, but six or seven can take it to places you never thought possible!

8. Raising Your Game

Ask any professional sportsman and you will learn that one of the best and quickest ways to improve your game is to play with better players or at least with players who will give you a strong challenge. The same is true in business, and participating in a mastermind group of successful business people will help you become a better business person yourself.

9. Resources & Connections

Everyone in your mastermind group is likely to have a different skill set or something that they are particularly strong at. For example, one might have had great success taking a business online and know things that you don't but that will be useful to your practice.

Of course, they are also all likely to know other useful businesses and people that you don't know, and this can open up whole new network of resources to you.

There is also a good opportunity for doing joint ventures with other businesses and promoting your practice to the clients and customers of the businesses owned by the other members. For example, if one of the members owned a beauty spa, you could run an offer to your clients and theirs offering grooming for dogs and beauty treatment for the women who own them. Alternatively, if one of the members owned a pet boutique, they might send out a mailing to their customers recommending your services; you would reciprocate at a later date.

10. New Friends, More Income!

It is said that your income is usually the average of the incomes of the five people who have the most influence in your life, the people you go to when you have a challenge or whose opinions you value the most. Doesn't it make sense therefore to make sure that the people whose opinions you value the most are doing well financially? Of course, having a whole group of new friends that you can talk business with might just be fun too!

Types Of Mastermind Group

Here are two types of mastermind group you should look to join to give your veterinary business a turbo boost:

1. Local Business Mastermind Groups

Local mastermind groups usually meet monthly at a local venue (e.g. a hotel, member's home, or private room in a local coffee shop), at the organizer's business, or in rotation at each of the members' businesses. Meetings can last from half a day to a whole day depending on the size of the group. A local business mastermind group should contain a mix of non-competing businesses such as CPAs, printers, beauty spas, doctors, dentists, etc.

You can find organized mastermind groups across the USA, for example, Glazer-Kennedy (www.dankennedy.com) runs mastermind groups in many US cities, and there are many other organizations that run local business mastermind groups. A quick Internet search for "mastermind group" with either your city or state should identify a few that you can choose from.

One note of warning, though: be careful not confuse mastermind groups with networking groups, as they are very different. Networking groups are usually much bigger, much less intimate, much shorter in duration, and much less able to work on any one individual's business. Networking groups are really more of a business to business event where contacts are made and business cards are exchanged.

2. Veterinary Mastermind Groups

The other type of mastermind group we recommend is a little harder to find but well worth joining. Whereas local business mastermind groups are made up of business owners representing different types of business, a veterinary mastermind group, as the name implies, is made up entirely of veterinary practice owners. Their meetings can be monthly but more often are less frequent because they are made up of veterinary practice owners from non-competing areas. While you might get on very well with the competing veterinarians in your area, you wouldn't want to tell them what your challenges are or what plans you have for being the most successful veterinary practice in the area!

The format of veterinary mastermind group meetings is very similar to local business mastermind group meetings, with the obvious exception and benefit that the focus is entirely on veterinary businesses. This means that virtually every second of discussion on every business in the group will be relevant to your business, so you should have pages of notes to take away with you.

Obviously, veterinary-specific meetings afford you the chance to discuss veterinary-specific issues, such as the latest medical equipment, for example, but the main focus should be on the growth of each of the veterinary businesses in the group.

If you want to accelerate your business growth, our advice is to get involved in a mastermind group as soon as possible. We run our own veterinary mastermind group, which meets quarterly, check out the website in the resources section of this book to enquire if there are any places currently available.

CHAPTER 23
PUTTING ON THE RITZ—GIVING YOUR CLIENTS AN EXPERIENCE TO REMEMBER

I've never felt like I was in the cookie business. I've always been in a feel good feeling business. My job is to sell joy. My job is to sell happiness. My job is to sell an experience.

–Debbi Fields

You now know how much testimonials and referrals can contribute to the growth of your veterinary practice, and you now know some strategies for acquiring them. You can make this process a whole lot easier for yourself, however, by creating a WOW Factor that makes your clients want to give referrals and testimonials before you've even asked for them.

So how do you create a WOW Factor? How can you turn a fairly ordinary experience like taking a pet to a veterinary clinic into a memorable experience that your clients will want to talk about to their pet-owning friends and family?

The Shortcut to 5-Star Client Care

The quickest way to achieve anything you want in life is to find someone who is achieving the results you want and imitate them.

For a model in delivering 5-star customer care, you need look no farther than the Ritz-Carlton Hotel Company. The lengths to which the Ritz-Carlton staff will go to assure their guests a memorable experience are legendary.

Every day, employees of every department in every Ritz-Carlton hotel around the world gather for a 15-minute staff meeting where they share WOW stories. These are real stories of how Ritz-Carlton employees have gone way above and beyond the usual level of hotel customer service.

The Internet is full of these legendary stories. There's the hotel chef who had special eggs and milk flown to Bali from a small grocery store in another country for a guest with food allergies.

There's the story about a honeymoon couple who had to change their booking from Hawaii to Los Angeles when the husband was diagnosed with cancer and scheduled for chemotherapy in LA. The story has it that when the hotel bartender heard their story, she immediately contacted the duty manager, and they decided that since the couple couldn't go to Hawaii, they would bring Hawaii to the couple.

They filled the couple's room with anything they could find that was reminiscent of Hawaii and left a complimentary bottle of Champagne in their room. They even reprogrammed a room key from the Hawaiian hotel so that it would work in the LA hotel room. That's what you call going the extra mile to give your clients an experience to remember!

Now, if you're thinking that the reason Ritz-Carlton can do these things is because they make millions of dollars each year, you're wrong. The reason they make millions is *because* they do these things! In a service industry, they differentiate themselves by providing extraordinary customer service.

It starts with a philosophy and culture of world-class service. On the Ritz-Carlton Website you will find the foundation of their success, what they call their Gold Standards.

They start with The Credo, which goes as follows:

The Ritz-Carlton Hotel is a place where the genuine care and comfort of our guests is our highest mission.

We pledge to provide the finest personal service and facilities for our guests who will always enjoy a warm, relaxed, yet refined ambience.

The Ritz-Carlton experience enlivens the senses, instills well-being, and fulfills even the unexpressed wishes and needs of our guests.

In Latin the word *credo* literally means *I Believe,* and this is something that is drummed into all Ritz-Carlton staff from day one.

What Does Your Staff Believe?

Take a moment and think what would be The Credo for your veterinary practice. Perhaps it might look something like this:

The XYZ Veterinary Practice is a place where first-class care, comfort, and veterinary medicine for our patients and first-class service and respect for our clients is our highest mission.

We pledge to provide the finest service and facilities for our clients and their pets, who will always enjoy a kind and friendly environment.

The XYZ Veterinary Practice experience conveys a love of animals, instills confidence in the care we provide, and delivers service beyond what our clients expect.

Three Steps of Service

Another of the Ritz-Carlton Gold Standards is what they call their Three Steps of Service, which are:

1. A warm and sincere greeting. Use the guest's name.

2. Anticipation and fulfillment of each guest's needs.

3. Fond farewell. Give a warm good-bye and use the guest's name.

You can see that it doesn't take a huge leap to transfer these steps to your veterinary practice. For example, how about this:

1. A warm and sincere greeting. Use the client's name and the pet's name.

2. Anticipation and fulfillment of each client's needs. Make the visit an experience to remember.

3. Fond farewell. Give a warm good-bye and use the client's name and the pet's name. Show your appreciation for their visit and express how much you

look forward to seeing them at their next appointment.

What Are Your Service Values?

Next, the Ritz-Carlton has what they call their Service Values that each member of staff must adhere to:

1. I build strong relationships and create Ritz-Carlton guests for life.

2. I am always responsive to the expressed and unexpressed wishes and needs of our guests.

3. I am empowered to create unique, memorable and personal experiences for our guests.

4. I understand my role in achieving the Key Success Factors, embracing Community Footprints and creating The Ritz-Carlton Mystique.

5. I continuously seek opportunities to innovate and improve The Ritz-Carlton experience.

6. I own and immediately resolve guest problems.

7. I create a work environment of teamwork and lateral service so that the needs of our guests and each other are met.

8. I have the opportunity to continuously learn and grow.

9. I am involved in the planning of the work that affects me.

10. I am proud of my professional appearance, language and behavior.

11. I protect the privacy and security of our guests, my fellow employees and the company's confidential information and assets.

12. I am responsible for uncompromising levels of cleanliness and creating a safe and accident-free environment.

Again, these are very transferable values for your staff members. We won't go through and create equivalents here because they are all pretty much relevant to your practice and you may want to add additional values.

We would, however, encourage you to visit the Ritz-Carlton Website to see the remainder of the Gold Standards (see Resources section).

What would the Gold Standards be in your veterinary practice?

Remember not to fall into the trap of thinking that a hotel group couldn't teach you anything about looking after your veterinary clients.

Implementation Is the Key!

Of course you can create Gold Standards for your practice, and they will look great on paper, but nothing will change in your practice unless you implement them.

With that in mind here are some practical things you can do immediately to implement Ritz-Carlton style Gold Standards in your veterinary practice:

Get Your Team on Board

Once you've developed your Gold Standards, have a team meeting and discuss why you're doing it and how it will benefit them. Implement the 15-minute daily meeting.

One of our clients locally has been having daily Ritz-Carlton style meetings for a few weeks now with great success. Each morning before the practice opens, they line up and discuss the day ahead. They know when problem clients are due and how to handle them; they know when long-term or high-value clients are due and what is expected by them.

Get Personal and Watch Your Clients Smile

We suggest taking it a stage further. As a matter of course, you should be taking the photo of every pet that joins your practice, and we suggest taking photos of clients with their pets, too.

Each day, the photos of clients due in that day should be available for your staff to review and sort into appointment order. The goal of this exercise is for your reception staff to recognize each client and pet and use the client's name before they hear it.

For example, can you imagine the reaction of the client who received the following greeting:

"Good morning, Mrs. Jones, it's good to see you and Rocky again. I believe Rocky is here for his annual check-up, how has he been since we last saw him?"

If Mrs. Jones hasn't been into the practice for twelve months, this recognition is going to blow her away.

Obviously if you haven't got the photos yet, then you can't

go as far as this, but this is where you should be aiming. In the meantime, make sure your staff at least look up the pet's name, the reason for the visit, the date of the last visit, and the reason for the last visit.

Then when the client arrives, the conversation might go like this:

"It's good to see you and Rocky again. How has Rocky been since he was here for his dental cleaning in March?"

When you start engaging with your clients in this very personal way, like they're longtime friends, they will not only appreciate it but tell their friends about it too.

A Smile Goes a Long Way

There's nothing worse for a client than being greeted by grumpy or surly receptionist. Sure, your team member might be having a bad day, but this might be the only time this year that your client will be in your practice. Do you really want the lasting impression to be of a miserable employee?

And don't think this doesn't affect a client's thinking when it comes to the revisit. We personally know pet owners who have moved veterinary practices because they were sick of being greeted by frown faced receptionists every time they visited!

As someone once said:

"A smile is the shortest distance between two people."

And nothing will create a connection and rapport with your clients more than a sincere, heartfelt smile. Notice the key words: sincere and heartfelt. A client can spot a fake smile a mile away, so a smile has to come from the heart and be sincere.

Empower Your Staff

It is important to resolve client issues as quickly as possible. A great way to do this is to give your staff the power to put things right immediately. Obviously, if it is a medical complaint, then it has to be you or one of your vets who remedies it. But the following scenario is more common:

Diet food is prescribed for a dog whose owner is given two brand options. A week later the client comes in to complain that the dog won't eat the chosen food. The client wants to return the opened bag. Instead of making the client wait while she speaks to the practice manager, the receptionist could be empowered to make the client happy instantly by making the exchange for a different brand at no cost.

Go the Extra Mile

It's often said that details make the difference, and this is certainly true when it comes to creating a world-class client experience.

For example, when a client has bought a large bag of dog food, or perhaps some other items that may be difficult to carry while keeping control of an animal, make sure you offer to assist. Your clients will love you for your thoughtfulness and appreciate your help.

Similarly, if it's raining outside when clients leave, make sure they're escorted with umbrellas to the parking lot. Ask your pharmaceutical or pet food sales representative to sponsor some umbrellas with your practice name on one side and their product name on the other. After the client is safe and dry in the vehicle, leave the umbrella as a souvenir of the event!

What other things can you do in your practice to go the extra mile and delight your clients? What are some courtesies they wouldn't expect but would rave about if you provided them?

How to WOW New Clients into Becoming Raving Fans from Day One.

In any walk of life, first impressions count a lot, and this is even more so in business.

There are some obvious places to make a good first impression, such as how your receptionists answer the telephone, how they greet arriving clients, the décor and condition of your premises, and the first experience with your veterinarians.

You should strive to create a WOW Factor in all of these areas, but there is a less obvious place to turn your clients into raving fans from day one. You can have them praising your practice all over town with the first piece of mail you send!

Here's a question: What do you send your new clients?

For most veterinary practices it's one of the following:

1. Nothing.

2. A formal letter welcoming them to the practice.

3. A letter welcoming them to the practice and enclosing a brochure (or folder containing promotional leaflets).

Do you think (in the case of 2 and 3) that when your clients receive this mail they think "Wow, that's awesome, I must tell my friends about that!"? Of course not; in fact most will just file it in the B1N folder (the trash can)!

Shock & Awe—Creating the WOW Factor!

So how do you create the WOW Factor with your first mailing? Well, try using a strategy we like to call Shock & Awe.

Why do we call it that? Because that's exactly how we want clients to feel when they receive it. We want them to be shocked (in a good way) at what they have received and be in such awe that they can't help but tell others about it.

So what is Shock & Awe?

Imagine the following scenario:

Your client has just visited your practice for the first time with Boomer, her Labrador puppy.

Your receptionists handled her original phone call and her visit with great care, friendliness, enthusiasm, and professionalism. So far so good!

Your veterinarians and technicians impressed her as knowledgeable, caring, and friendly. Even better!

A few days later your client receives a mysterious package in the mail. The gift tag says, "A special gift for Boomer and his Mom." Your client rarely receives gifts by mail, so this is a pleasant surprise and a welcome change from the usual utility bills, catalogs and never ending credit card solicitations.

She unwraps the package and discovers the following:

- A welcome letter from your practice.

- A DVD containing a tour of your practice, a personal welcome from you, interviews with your vets, and video testimonials from your clients.

- A refrigerator magnet printed with your practice details.
- A booklet entitled "The Happy Pets of XYZ Veterinary Practice," containing photos and stories about successful treatments.
- A booklet written by you and your vets on preventative care for her dog and how it can save her money.
- A booklet containing pet-friendly recipes.
- A pack of dog food.
- Some dog chews.
- A squeaky toy.
- A gift card to use at your boarding kennels or grooming parlor.
- A refrigerator magnet photo frame with Boomer's photo in it (your technicians took a photo of Boomer during the visit).
- Some referral vouchers to give to other pet owners that reward her for referring with gift cards for local restaurants and spas.
- A chocolate brownie for the owner to eat with her coffee while going through the shock & awe box!

After going through the box she is shocked at the amount of stuff she has received (she's never had this treatment from any of the other vets she's visited) and in awe of what a great veterinary clinic she has joined. Boomer is happy too, and she is feeling great at sharing the experience with him.

The phone rings and it's her best friend, who also happens to own a dog. What do you think is the first thing they talk about?

She then has her daily half hour on Facebook, where 30 of her pet-owning friends are following her posts. Do you think your practice might just get a mention in her daily news?

That's Shock & Awe!

Compare this experience, and by the way, that's exactly what this creates for the client—an experience—with what happens at most veterinary practices.

From a typical practice, the client receives an envelope containing a standard welcome letter or even a brochure... The client opens the letter... It's the same standard stuff sent by every other vet... After a quick glance it gets filed or put into the trash. Do you think this letter will get mentioned to anyone? Not very likely!

That's Flop & Bore!

Now you may be thinking that putting together a Shock & Awe package for each new client sounds like a lot of work, and you'd be correct in that assumption. But that's exactly why you should do it, because your competitors will think the very same thing (*It's too much work.*) and won't even attempt it.

The clients who have taken our advice and implemented Shock & Awe packages are getting great feedback from their clients. You can too if you dare to be different and try it in your practice.

Birth of a Raving Fan

The great author and management expert Ken Blanchard

wrote in his best-selling book *Raving Fans*, "If you really want to 'own' a customer, if you want a booming business, you have to go beyond satisfied customers and create Raving Fans."

Having raving fans means that you have achieved the kind of service excellence that turns a customer into a lifetime customer. A raving fan is an advocate of your products or services in the marketplace.

The first step to creating a raving fan is to give your client a world-class experience.

Creating a world-class client experience starts with your first interactions, and a Shock & Awe package helps set the tone from day one.

Referrals and Testimonials from Day One

Of course, once you have created raving fans, they will happily provide you with two of the most powerful yet inexpensive ways to market your veterinary practice...Referrals and Testimonials.

A raving fan will be a keen and active participant in your referral programs and competitions and will also give unsolicited plugs for your practice to anyone who so much as mentions the word pet!

The raving fan also will be at the front of the line to give you a testimonial. Referrals and Testimonials should be good enough reasons to create the Shock & Awe package for new clients, but there are some other compelling reasons.

Differentiation and Positioning

Remember, every potential new client is wondering, "Why should I choose your veterinary practice over every other veterinary practice available to me?"

As we said at the beginning of this book, to answer that question and to survive and thrive in the New Economy you must create a USP (Unique Selling Proposition) for your practice. You must find ways to differentiate yourself from your competition and position yourself against your competition.

Sending the Shock & Awe package to new clients should be one of the ways achieve this. It differentiates you from your competitors because it's something they won't be doing. It helps position your practice as a world-class facility providing a world-class client experience.

If you're targeting affluent pet owners as clients, which you should be, then a Shock & Awe package is very congruent with that market and will assure them that they've come to the right place.

The Costs of Shock & Awe

Now you may be thinking that this Shock & Awe stuff sounds expensive, but it isn't.

The DVDs and booklets are inexpensive to create, promotional items such as fridge magnets cost very little, and everything else is something you should be buying anyway. An impressive Shock & Awe package could cost you less than $25, but even if it cost $50, it would still be money well spent.

How? Because the average annual veterinary expenditure of a client in the USA is about $400, which means you'll get back your investment—including the marketing cost to acquire the client in the first place—in the first year.

However, it shouldn't end there. The impact of Shock &

Awe should result in your clients being with you for many years to come and bringing you many more new clients over the course of those years.

Of course, the other benefit is that our aim for you is not to be average. If you have been implementing our strategies, the average annual spend of your clients should be significantly more than $400.

Think of the items that you can put in your Shock & Awe package, what the package would look like, and what your investment per client would be. Find a source for each item, the create a system for ensuring that every new client gets a package.

Dare to Be Different

The biggest single thing you can do to survive and thrive in the New Economy is to be different because if you do the same as every other veterinary practice, then you'll get the same results.

Remember: you can distinguish yourself by delivering a world-class client experience. That will make you practically recession-proof because you are not just better than everybody else, you are so much different than everyone else.

Which means…

- You will attract more quality clients.
- You will have better client retention.
- You will be able to raise your fees.
- You will get more referrals.

- You will enjoy increased client trust.
- You will attain financial freedom!

So here's the question:

Do you dare to be different?

To become a Master you must NEVER stop being a Student.

–Steve Maughan & Dean Biggs

SECTION 6

Resources & Useful Information

Other useful resources for growing your veterinary practice.

USEFUL RESOURCES

This section contains some useful resources you can use to get more information on some of the topics we introduced in this book.

Books

The New Economy
No B.S. Wealth Attraction in the New Economy by Dan Kennedy
No B.S. Business Success in The New Economy by Dan Kennedy

Mindset
Think & Grow Rich by Napoleon Hill
Eat That Frog By Brian Tracy
Goals by Brian Tracy

Entrepreneurship
The E-Myth Revisited By Michael E Gerber
The E-Myth Physician By Michael E Gerber

Direct Response Marketing
The Ultimate Sales Letter By Dan Kennedy
The Ultimate Marketing Plan By Dan Kennedy

Advertising
Scientific Advertising By Claude Hopkins
My Life in Advertising By Claude Hopkins
Tested Advertising Methods By John Caples

Websites

3D/Lumpy Mail - www.3DMailResults.com
Copywriting – www.simplewritingsystem.com
Tear Sheets - www.specializedmailing.com
Dan Kennedy - www.dankennedy.com
Brian Tracy - www.briantracy.com
Ritz-Carlton (Gold standards) –

http://corporate.ritzcarlton.com/en/about/goldstandards.htm
The Barkley Pet Hotel – www.thebarkleypethotel.com

Auto responders – www.aweber.com
www.MailChimp.com
www.constantcontact.com
www.officeautopilot.com
www.infusionsoft.com

Social Media – www.facebook.com
www.twitter.com
www.youtube.com
www.posterous.com

Blogging Software – www.wordpress.com

Veterinary Specific

www.Easy4Vets.com
'Done For You' Client Newsletters, Direct Response Marketing Campaigns and Website Client Attraction Systems.

www.VeterinaryMastermindGroup.com
Facilitated, Accelerated Learning & Application Of Marketing And Business Success Strategies in a group environment with other non-competing veterinary practice owners.

www.VeterinaryInsidersClub.com
Get real 'How-To' strategies on growing your veterinary practice delivered to your mailbox every month including the 'Passport To Veterinary Practice Profits' Newsletter, Audio CD and marketing resource.

ABOUT THE AUTHORS

Steve Maughan

Steve has over fifteen years of experience in the animal health business. He has worked with three of the world's top five animal health companies and in over thirty countries worldwide.

Steve is an Honors Graduate from Cambridge University in England and now lives near Orlando, Florida, with his wife and two daughters.

Dean Biggs

Dean is a marketing expert with over fifteen years experience as a small business owner. He is an expert in Internet marketing and advises veterinarians on how to make the Internet work for them.

Dean resides in Lake Mary, Florida, with his wife, daughter, and two miniature smooth-haired dachshunds.

Their Easy4Vets "Done For You" Marketing Program, their monthly Veterinary Insiders Club™, and their prestigious Veterinary Mastermind Program are just some of the ways Steve and Dean work together to help veterinary practice owners across America grow their businesses.

For more details visit **www.VetPracticeProfits.com**

INDEX

K

L

M

N

O

P

Q

R

S

T

U

V

W

Y

43741538R00147

Made in the USA
Middletown, DE
18 May 2017